Praise for Homer's Odyssey

"Touching...one not to miss."

—*USA Today*

"This memoir about adopting a special-needs kitten teaches that sometimes in life, you have to take a blind leap."

—*People*

"Cooper is a genial writer with a gift for conveying the inner essence of an animal."

—*The Christian Science Monitor*

"Delightful...This lovely human-feline memoir, following in the footsteps of Vicki Myron's bestselling *Dewey: The Small-Town Library Cat Who Touched the World*, is sure to warm the hearts of all pet lovers."

—*Library Journal*

"Well written with...tenderness and realism...Your life will be richer for having taken this journey with [Gwen and Homer]."

—*I Love Cats* magazine

Praise for My Life in a Cat House

"This book perfectly encapsulates the unique and amazing experience of being owned by cats and the joy they bring into our lives. That alone is reason enough to read it."

—James Bowen, international bestselling author of *A Street Cat Named Bob*

"Cooper, who charmed readers with the best-selling memoir of her intrepid blind cat, *Homer's Odyssey*, returns with escapades of other past and present felines. Cooper's witty, breezy writing, her unabashed love of felines, and her admission that her spoiled cats have trained her will delight and resonate with cat people."

—*Library Journal*

"Fans of *Homer's Odyssey* will rejoice upon hearing that Homer's owner, Cooper, has returned with more true cat stories...both hilarious and deeply moving. Readers...will delight in these anecdotes of cats who seemingly have something to say about everything. Fans of Vicky Myron and Brett Witter's *Dewey* and James Bowen's *A Street Cat Named Bob* will be highly satisfied."

—*Booklist*

"If you've ever lived with a cat, then this book is for you ... In *My Life in a Cat House,* Cooper lovingly and humorously depicts the ups and downs of a life with cats and the ways in which they mimic human behavior and feelings. A fun read for all animal lovers."

—*New York Journal of Books*

"A literary fur fix for Homer fans!"

—*Catster* magazine

"As Gwen shares the joys, sorrows, laughter and tears of sharing her life with her cats, both past and present, you will find yourself nodding in recognition and perhaps remember the antics of a cat long gone. You may even gain a deeper understanding of your own feline companions."

—The Conscious Cat

"Gwen has the uncanny ability to touch our hearts with her gift of conveying thought-provoking and heart-stirring emotions...Gwen's writing is unpretentious, it's authentic, it's REAL. Whether like me you have nearly all of Gwen's books, or if this one is your first, you will delight in her descriptive, often hilarious and loving stories about her cats."

—Cat Chat with Caren and Cody

"There's something about Gwen Cooper's cat books that touch my heart like few others, and *My Life in a Cat House* is no exception. Whether you've enjoyed every one of Gwen's cat books or this is your first, snuggle up with a cat or two while you're reading. I guarantee with each turn of the page you'll pull them just a little bit closer as you realize just how empty your life would be without their unconditional love."

—Melissa's Mochas, Mysteries and Meows

"Gwen Cooper is the Queen of Cat Love—and in these fun and frisky stories, she perfectly captures all the reasons felines rule our hearts and our homes. No cat lover should be without this book, but more important, give it to the folks who haven't yet seen the light. At least they'll understand us better!"

—Sy Montgomery, bestselling author of *How to Be a Good Creature: A Memoir in Thirteen Animals*

"What a pleasure to read [Gwen Cooper's] beautiful stories, brimming with her cat-love and even more important her ability to get you to actually see her cats . . . You will want to see more and more. She can become your next obsession, as she has become mine!"

—Jeffrey Moussaieff Masson, international bestselling author of *The Nine Emotional Lives of Cats*

Praise for Love Saves the Day

"Prudence is a sassy but sensitive feline heroine."

—Time

"Once again Gwen Cooper shines her light on the territory that defines the human/animal bond."

—Jackson Galaxy, star of *My Cat From Hell*

"Hauntingly beautiful, heart touching, and at times painfully raw. This book will stay with you long after you turn the final page."

—The Conscious Cat

Also by Gwen Cooper

Homer's Odyssey: A Fearless Feline Tale, or How I Learned About Love and Life with a Blind Wonder Cat

Homer: The Ninth Life of a Blind Wonder Cat

Homer and the Holiday Miracle

Spray Anything: More True Tale of Homer & the Gang

My Life in a Cat House: True Tales of Love, Laughter, and Living with Five Felines

The 10th Anniversary Homer's Odyssey *Scrapbook*

YOU are PAWSOME! 75 Reasons Why Your Cats Love You, and Why Loving Them Back Makes You a Better Human

THE BOOK OF PAWSOME

*Head Bonks, Raspy Tongues,
and 101 Reasons Why Cats
Make Us So, So Happy*

GWEN COOPER

Originally published in paperback in the United States by Interrobang Books as *The Book of PAWSOME! Head Bonks, Raspy Tongues, and 101 Reasons Why Cats Make Us So, So Happy* in 2020.

Cooper, Gwen.
PAWSOME: Head bonks, raspy tongues, and 101 reasons why cats make us so, so happy.
ISBN 979-8643284161

Nonfiction; humor; pets

Illustrations by Jessica Rodrigue
Cover design by 100 Covers

Foreword

I t was back in mid-February of 2020—almost exactly one month to the day before the world began to shut down—when I was browsing through a bookstore and spotted a title that, despite its having been a big bestseller, I'd never heard of.

It was by someone named Neil Parischa and was called *The Book of Awesome: Snow Days, Bakery Air, Finding Money in Your Pocket, and Other Simple, Brilliant Things.* From a marketing perspective it was a brilliant title, insofar as I immediately and intuitively grasped what the book was about. And, just as immediately, I wondered, *Why isn't there a Book of PAWsome about cats?*

And so it was that this book was born.

There aren't any hard-and-fast rules governing either the specific entries or the lengths of those entries in this book, aside from my gut feeling that each entry is as long or short as it ought to be. The entries in the first section, however—which is dedicated to capturing the joy in specific moments *with* cats, as opposed to certain qualities that cats have—tend to be a bit shorter.

I also tried to avoid being too "explain-y" for the most part. There are plenty of books out there that will tell you the whys and where-fores about the ways in which cats behave, and I wasn't seeking to duplicate their efforts.

Last but not least, I also made a commitment to playing it straight. In other words, while this book is certainly (raspy) tongue-in-cheek, it's never sarcastic. Even when an entry seems to dwell on one of the very few alleged "negatives" of living with a cat—the way, for example, a cat will rip up toilet paper just when it's become *extremely* difficult to find—I, personally, am always more genuinely tickled than annoyed when my cats shred paper goods. And since it's something cats do that makes me laugh, I included it in the book.

Ultimately, what I hope is that you, too, will enjoy a good chuckle when you read these pages, and find a little of the joy in everyday things—and in every day we get to spend with our cats—that can sometimes seem elusive. I'm an incurable optimist, something I inherited from my grandmother, and I always do believe that, with our cats by our sides, better days lie ahead for all of us.

Optimism is also something I get from my cats, who never seem less than 100% certain that another bag of Greenies is waiting for them at the end of the rainbow...

PAWSOME!

Contents

Days of Heaven

*Those little moments of **PAWSOME**
that cat lovers live for...*

When your cat is completely hidden under the bed...except for the little tail that's sticking out

"**I**f I can't see *you*, then you can't see *me*!"

PAWSOME!

When your cat pats you very gently with her paw to get your attention

C ats have a reputation for being "aloof" and "standoffish" creatures—and it may often seem as if that reputation is well
earned. But anybody who's lived with a cat knows that sometimes
they're actually quite desperate for human attention.

Not that *acting* desperate is in a cat's nature. Heavens no! Rather,
cats tend to prefer the subtle approach.

If it were another person trying to get your attention, they might
holler your name or shoot over a buzzing and intrusive text message.
An enthusiastic dog might bark and whine and jump at you until
you were forced to look up from your book, or perhaps relinquish a
morsel of food from your plate, as an act of simple self-preservation.

But cats are exquisitely courteous when they wish to be. A cat
who's hoping to draw your eyes from that book, or score a tempting
table tidbit, likely won't shriek or leap at you. Holding his desperate
impulses in check, your cat will instead very gently and respectfully
pat your shoulder or leg a few times with his velvety front paw (claws
retracted, of course) until you finally look his way. Almost as if he
were saying: "I'm *terribly* sorry, old chap, but if it wouldn't be *too*
much trouble to give me your attention for *just* a moment..."

It's the politeness of it that always kills me.

So terribly well-mannered. More than a little endearing. And
oh-so-very
PAWSOME!

When you wake up early on a Sunday morning to feed your cat and realize you can get back into bed for another two or three hours

Waking up in the mornings to a fuzzy, whiskered snout rubbing gently against your face is infinitely better than being jarred into the day by the grating buzzer of an alarm clock, as any cat lover will tell you.

The problem, however, and as the old saying goes, is that there's no snooze button on a hungry cat. If your cat is used to getting breakfast at 6:00 a.m. while you begin your mad scramble of showering, making up, and dressing before flying out the door for your workday commute, then 6:00 a.m. is when your cat will expect to be fed *every* morning—even on Sundays, the one day out of the whole week when you can lie about as late as you want to, like you were the Queen of England.

Still, there's something to be said for being awakened for breakfast of a Sunday morning by your impatient cat and then realizing—after your cat has been fed—that *you can get back into bed* and stay there for hours, blissfully inert. Maybe you catch some more Z's. Maybe you turn on your bedroom TV to that basic cable station that plays Sunday-morning reruns of your all-time favorite shows. Maybe you just wrap yourself up in your warm blanket, flip your pillow over to the cool side, and snuggle in, thinking: *This is the life!* Chances are your furry bestie will improve an already *purr*fect scenario by joining you for that excellent Sunday bonus nap, once her hunger has been sated.

The point is, you can spend an extra three or four idyllic hours in one of the best places in the whole world—your very own bed—re-awaken in plenty of time to throw on sweats and beat the Sunday-morning rush at your favorite pancake joint (having a semi-empty diner nearly all to yourself on a Sunday morning is *soooooo great!*), and *still* have an entire lazy Sunday in front of you when you finally emerge, happily stuffed with pancakes, the sweetness of melted butter and maple syrup warm on your tongue.

If it weren't for your cat, you would have slept all the way through those golden hours of self-indulgence. You would have missed out on that fifth re-viewing of Season 3 *Mad Men* from the comfort of your bed, followed by bacon and flapjacks. You would have woken up hours later, bleary-eyed and bewildered because you blew right past your usual wake-up time. You would've opened your eyes to full, disorienting daylight, along with the alarmed feeling of *Did I oversleep?!!?* before remembering that it's Sunday—an entire glorious day off that, sadly, is now already halfway gone, before you got a chance to bask fully in Sunday-morning delights.

But that didn't happen to you. *You*, you lucky human, were able to add a joyfully languid three or four hours onto your already leisurely Sunday, and it's all thanks to the purring bundle of love cuddled up next to you in the bed.

And that's **PAWSOME!**

When cats wiggle their butts before they pounce

Nobody's sure why cats wiggle their butts before they pounce. Theories range from it being a type of kitty calisthenics (to warm up their muscles before a leap), a way of getting a firmer foothold before launching an attack, a method of adding greater momentum to a jump, and possibly a way of focusing a cat's attention.

Then again, why ask why? It's hilarious, it's hella fun to watch, and ultimately we have only one thing to say on the subject:

Shake it like a Polaroid picture, kitty!

PAWSOME!

When you bring home a new kind of cat food, and your cat actually likes it!

W e've all been there. Maybe the pet store has run out of Mr. Whiskers' favorite flavor of food. Maybe the manufacturer discontinued it. Maybe there's a food that your cat absolutely *loved* as recently as yesterday, but today when you put it down, Mr. Whiskers not only refused to touch it, he gave you the sulky stink-eye all afternoon.

(*But you loved it YESTERDAY!* A cry from the cat lover's very soul.)

The only thing you can ever really know for sure about cats is that their decision-making process is ultimately unknowable—which means you're pretty much just groping in the dark on those occasions when circumstances force you to seek out a new flavor of food for your kitty's consumption. *He always enjoys tuna...I guess that's close enough to mackerel to give it a shot?*

Sadly, when you finally get that new brand or flavor of food home—and set it before your finicky feline as anxiously as an aspiring singer auditioning for an industry legend—your only likely reward for all the time and careful deliberation you've invested will be an upturned nose and the sight of your cat's backside stalking away.

But, every so often, the stars align just right—and Mr. Whiskers actually *likes* the new flavor! The little mound of food in the dish gets smaller and smaller until there's nothing but empty dish left—and beside that empty dish Mr. Whiskers is now luxuriously and elaborately cleaning his snout, which is the feline equivalent of lighting a cigarette and unbuckling your belt following a thoroughly satisfying meal.

You did it! Yippee!!!!!!!!!!!!

Now you don't have a thing in the world to worry about—at least, not until the pet store runs out of this food, as well.

PAWSOME!

When you buy your cat a new toy, and she actually plays with it!

C at toys are a suckers' game. You stand in front of that colorful display in the pet store full of hope and enthusiasm, trying to determine exactly which of the bouncing, buzzing, rolling, springing, or airborne gizmos in front of you will best tempt your opinionated tabby into cavorting delightfully around the living room for, perhaps, as long as five completely entertaining minutes. *This time, I've done it*, you think, as you walk out of the pet store clutching a shopping bag filled with dollar-ninety-eight treasures. You're as proud as a Viking carrying sacks of gold and other spoils of battle back to your homeland and lady-love, ready to throw them at her feet as you assure yourself that, *This time I've found at least one toy that Fluffy will love!*

When you arrive home with that pet-store bag in your hand, however, you realize just how futile those hopes were. Fussy little Fluffy is certainly very interested in the *bag* that the toy came in. Ah, the endless possibilities of a bag! A cat can sleep on top of a bag, or turn a bag into a just-her-size makeshift cave, or chew a bag to bits, leaving a trail of itty-bitty bag scraps strewn on the floor all around her.

But the toy itself—this object to which you've affixed your dreams of glory, and on the selection of which you expended at least a good fifteen or twenty minutes—is sniffed at for perhaps all of four seconds. Then it's ignored completely, left to make its slow, sad voyage to the toy graveyard that accumulates in one corner of the living room until it's time for spring cleaning, when all the unsuccessful toys are looked at one last time (farewell, rubber ball with feather attached; we hardly knew ye, cotton-stuffed striped goldfish) before being tossed out with the trash.

Still, statisticians tell us that, on a long enough timeline, anything that *can* happen *will* happen. So, every so often, through the sheer law of averages, you hit by chance upon a toy that your cat actually *likes*! The glory of it! Your cat sniffs at the toy, perhaps suspiciously at first. (*What fresh hell is this?*) But then suspicion gives way to curiosity, curiosity turns to playfulness, and finally—miracle of miracles!—Fluffy cavorts, she capers, she leaps and dips and spins with glee. She races across the room to fling herself on the couch, dragging her brand-new and already beloved toy with her, where she proceeds to claw it, bite it, maul it, and eventually nap right next to it for the next several hours at least.

YOU DID IT!!!

For perhaps an entire afternoon—maybe even as long as one whole week!—Fluffy is fascinated with the goods that the gods...or, y'know, *you*...have seen fit to provide her. And *you* get to strut proudly and triumphantly around the house like the conquering hero you are.

PAWSOME!

When you see your cat sleeping in a pool of sunlight

E very so often, on a sunny spring day, when I walk into a room to find one of my cats sprawled out and blissfully asleep in a pool of sunlight streaming through the window—every strand of fur illuminated and glowing like a halo—a feeling of pure peacefulness cups my heart.

Do you know that feeling?

And, if it's a black cat, sometimes you even catch a glimpse of a chocolate-brown or tabby-striped undercoat that remains hidden most of the time.

So beautiful. So, so **PAWSOME.**

When your cat gives you the heavy-lidded look of, "I love you soooooo much..."

There are "experts" who say that, because cats have fewer muscles around their eyes than dogs do, their faces are therefore less expressive.

Don't believe it for one second.

Anyone who's lived with a cat for any length of time is familiar with *the look*. You know the one I'm talking about: that eyes-half-closed gaze of *purr*fect adoration your cat will sometimes bestow upon you—when he half-wakes from a particularly excellent nap to the gentle touch of your hand; when your fingers have managed to find that one spot to scratch behind his ears that's *juuuuuuuuuust* right; when you're standing in the kitchen chopping vegetables and, for no particular reason, he comes in to stand beside you, flicks his tail around your lower leg, and turns his head to gaze up at you with his whole heart in his eyes.

You might only see that gaze in your cat's eyes for a moment—but it's a moment that will stick with you for the rest of your life.

PAWSOME!

When your cat stands on his hind legs like a meerkat

S o doofy. So adorable. So unbelievably...

PAWSOME!

When your cat gets into a life-and-death battle with a piece of lint

O ne of the greatest things about cats is that they have such vivid imaginations.

Sadly, it's impossible for cats to tell us the stories they make up in their heads. Still, we have ample evidence of their epic fantasy lives on full display before our very eyes.

It's evident, for example, when your cat *veeeeeeeeeery* slowly sneaks up on some inanimate toy that, y'know, can't actually *see* her coming. It's clear that, in your cat's mind, however, that harmless-looking plaything is actually a mortal foe—one crafty enough that your intrepid feline has to execute a careful stealth attack to give herself the tactical advantage of surprise. *Well, well, Dr. Felt-Mouse...so we meet again...*

But never is this abundant imagination on greater display than when your cat is embroiled in a rolled-on-her-back, bunny-feet-kicking, *battle royale* to the death with...well, it's hard to tell. A shifty-looking gnat? A piece of lint that got a little too mouthy?

Watching your cat stage an epic mêlée with nothing in particular is a wonderful and constant reminder of what it felt like to be a kid—a harkening back to days when you didn't need much more to conjure up entertainment than your own imagination.

PAWSOME!

When your cat puts two paws on your chest and very sweetly asks to be petted

C ats take a lot of ribbing for being stubborn, opinionated, temperamental, aloof, lazy, erratic, and more.

(Honestly, though, who among *isn't* most of those things sometimes? For me, personally, it's a good day when I'm only one or two of them.)

But the closely guarded secret known only to cat lovers is that cats can, more often than not, be such incredible little *loves*. Like when you're just hanging out on the couch watching TV or reading a book, and your cat suddenly springs up next to you, rises up on her hind legs, then very gently (and very sweetly) places her two front paws on your chest in an unmistakable *please pet me* request.

Maybe she even raises her head to touch her little nose to yours.

There's only word in the English language capable of describing the utter, heart-melting adorableness of such moments: *Awwwwwwwwwwwww...*

Actually, make that two:

PAWSOME!

When your cat "follows" you from the front

I t's incredibly endearing when your cat is so enamored of your presence that he eagerly follows you from room to room.

But what's even cuter than *that* is when your cat is just so gosh-darn thrilled to be with you that he's too giddy and impatient to actually wait while you go from one room to the other. Instead, he races out ahead of you—but remains close enough to turn his head back from time to time to make sure you're still right there with him. And his ears will turn back, too—just to keep extra tabs on you.

It's as if every inch of his body is crying out, *Let's hurry up and get there so we can cuddle already!*

My cat Homer used to do this all the time.

It's thoroughly adorable, completely loving, and absolutely **PAWSOME!**

When you hug your cat and he smells like cookies

This may be too specific to apply to most cats, because it's something I've personally experienced with only one of the cats I've lived with. But my cat Homer sometimes smelled like cookies. Or, to be precise, the back of his neck occasionally gave off a very distinct aroma that always made me think of my childhood, and of afternoons at the kitchen table with a plate of warm cinnamon cookies and a tall, cool glass of milk to dunk them in.

Homer was only a tiny kitten the first time when, while cuddling him, I caught a whiff of cinnamon and milk. I wondered briefly if I might be experiencing some sort of apoplexy, because I'd read somewhere that smelling oranges, for example, when there weren't any oranges around might be a sign you were having a stroke. But over the next few months I noticed that same comforting smell a few more times when I picked Homer up or affectionately buried my nose in the scruff of his neck, which seemed to argue against the "it's a stroke" theory.

For years, I assumed that a tendency to smell like baked goods was unique to Homer—an additional special quality in a cat already special in so many ways. I wasn't even entirely sure that it wasn't all in my head, since I usually noticed the fragrance most strongly when I was feeling down or in especial need of Homer's comfort.

But nearly two decades later, while working on a book about him, I described in some detail this particularly endearing trait, and my cat-loving copy editor dropped in the following note while reviewing the manuscript: *I know exactly what you mean! My Jasper smelled just like my mom's vanilla coconut cookies!*

So there you have it. If I were a betting woman (full disclosure: I find gambling to be intensely stressful), I'd wager that somewhere out there are even more cat ladies and cat dudes who can report similar phenomena. Lovers of cookie-smelling cats, unite!

One of my favorite network shows in recent years was *The Good Place*, an NBC sitcom about a woman who winds up in Heaven by mistake. In one episode, it's explained that Heaven smells different for everyone, depending on what their favorite smell was while they were alive on Earth.

If that turns out to be true, then I know exactly what Heaven's fragrance will be for me. When the pearly gates open wide to take me in, wafting through them will be the aroma of a little blind, black cat—a cat who somehow, mysteriously, smelled just like fresh cinnamon cookies right out of the oven...

PAWSOME!

When your cat slow-blinks at you

No less a person than world-famous cat behaviorist Jackson Galaxy has said that when a cat slowly blinks at you—not just a regular blink, but a very deliberate and languid slow-blink of the eyes—it's essentially a feline way of saying, "I love you."

Cats are predators, but they're also prey, and are therefore reluctant to show their vulnerabilities. So when your cat slow-blinks at you, he's basically letting you know that he feels very safe and comfortable in your presence—so safe and comfortable, in fact, that he's able to close his eyes for a moment, knowing that you can be completely trusted.

Cats aren't exactly known for their blind faith in others, and the number of people (or other cats) that the typical feline trusts completely is usually very, *very* small. So having successfully earned the trust of a cat isn't an accomplishment that anybody should take lightly.

In fact, it's pretty **PAWSOME!**

When your cat sleeps with one paw over her eyes

E verybody has their own opinion as to which of a cat's sleeping positions is the absolute cutest. And while there's a great deal to be said for Sprawled On Back With Tummy Showing, or Curled Up In Ball With Tail Covering Nose, for my money I'll take Paw Over Eyes every day of the week and twice on Sunday.

Usually a cat with her paw over her eyes will be partially rolled onto her side, which means you still get to see a good bit of mushy tummy—although, granted, not all of it. But what you lose in belly fluff, you more than make up for in paw. Cats' velvety-soft little paws are a great deal of their charm, but rarely do you get the unobstructed view of teeny-tiny toe beans that the Paw Over Eyes sleeping position offers.

And there's something so touching and almost *human* about a cat sleeping with one paw flung casually across her face. I'm not necessarily an adherent to the "cats are little people in fur suits" school of thought but, at such moments, I'm halfway there.

Ultimately, though, it probably pays not to try to dissect the cuteness of it too much. Rather, we should simply accept these gifts of adorableness wherever we find them, and agree that it's indisputably **PAWSOME!**

When your cat plays with running water

Cats have a general aversion to water that's well known even among people who know little else about cats. And, indeed, it's tough to imagine a sadder sight than that of a bedraggled, soaking wet, and thoroughly discomfited cat (poor little thing!).

But while most cats (with a few breed exceptions) might not like *immersing* themselves in water—and while the typical cat on a wet-food diet might even avoid drinking too much water—that doesn't mean they have no interest in liquids whatsoever.

Your cat might be fascinated with watching water run out of a flushing toilet bowl, for example. Or she might show a lively interest in running water straight from the tap.

Even some cats who are water-shy for the most part will find it fascinating when it's running out of a faucet. Experts say that a cat might prefer drinking from a tap to drinking from a bowl because running tap water is fresher and more oxygenated. Regardless of the reason, seeing that sideways kitty head tilt—a bid to give their little pink tongue a better lapping angle—never fails to tickle me.

Even cuter is the way some cats will "wash" their paws in running water—although, here again, experts will chime in to sathe reason they're doing that is to filter the water through the strands of fur on their paws. So, nature's answer to a Brita, basically, rather than an attempt to mimic human habits of hand sanitation.

Nevertheless, it's still *paws*itively adorable!

Pro tip: A great way to get your cat to drink more water (most cats would benefit from being a tad more hydrated) while also upping your amusement factor is to buy your pampered puss his very own cat fountain. You can find tons of reasonably priced options on Amazon or at your local pet store.

Then just plug that bad boy in, fill it with water, and immerse yourself in the **PAWSOME**!

When your cat tries to squeeze into a too-small cardboard box

You will never love anything the way your cat loves a cardboard box.

He'll love it whether it's been dyed deep crimson or remains plain cardboard brown; whether it has fancy writing on its sides or no design at all; whether it's brand spanking new or has been lying around in an attic for the better part of a decade.

And he'll love that box even if it's way too big or too small to provide maximum kitty comfort.

Watching a cat trying to squeeze himself into a cardboard box that's far, *far* too small is *far* more entertaining than it should be. It's like watching a mean-spirited society matron at Saks trying to shove a size-ten foot into a size-six pump. It's like watching all those circus clowns who come pouring out of the tiny clown car trying to stuff themselves back into it.

Not too many things will make you laugh harder, in other words—and if it's been too long since you've seen this particular bit of comedy gold play out in your own home, then maybe it's time to order a book from Amazon post-haste, just so you can get one of those little boxes they send out single books in.

When your book arrives, you know exactly what to do: Remove book from box, set that itty-bitty box out on your living room floor, call your cat over...

And let the **PAWSOME** begin!

When your cat chases shimmers and sunbeams up the wall

I t's an odd quirk of the human/feline relationship that the more a cat stares at something with plainly murderous intent, the more adorable we find said cat to be.

I'm not talking about songbirds or pet gerbils or anything that's, y'know, *alive*. I mean when we see a cat giving the all-pupils Murder Look to a Christmas-tree ornament, or the ballerina figurine atop a little girl's birthday cake, or even a small stuffed animal.

Harmless things. *Pretty* things. And yet, the prettier and more harmless the prospective "victim" is in this scenario, the more we coo delightedly as we watch Bootsie hunker down and prepare to leap in full KILL-CRUSH-DESTROY mode at a festive scrap of giftwrap paper. *Who's mommy's little predator? Who's my fuzzy-wuzzy wizzle killer?*

Among the very prettiest things your cat will do her absolute level best to murder for your amusement are the shimmers that fall through windows onto walls and floors on a sunny day. They might be rainbow-colored and cast by a prism hanging from a window frame, or simply the ghostly-white result of light striking a reflective surface at a certain angle—a glass coffee table, perhaps, or the face of your cell phone.

I will freely confess that, in my house, the light shimmers are often created on purpose by me—deliberately toggling my glasses back and forth in the light—just because it's so much *fun* to watch my cats track its progress up the wall, across the ceiling, and back down an opposite wall. (Watching both their heads crane up at identical angles and move from left to right in perfect sync—like two little sunflowers—kills me every single time.) Their eyes become *enormous*, and they crouch down low on their hind legs until the tension is nearly unbearable—at which point they spring directly at the wall and the light shimmer they've been tracking, only to discover that their paws are empty.

My cats have been doing this for years now, and the fact that they've never once succeeded in pinning down a light shimmer and killing the heck out of it doesn't seem to have taken one particle of fun out of the game for them—or made it one iota less entertaining for me to watch.

The light shimmer is an illusion, of course. There's no possible way for them ever to catch it. Nevertheless, their hope that maybe *this* time they'll finally get their paws around that elusive prize burns as bright as the sun that casts the shimmers they chase.

In this, my cats display an optimism well worth emulating.
PAWSOME!

When your cat leans hard into your hand during a scritching session

D o cats enjoy receiving head scritches more than we like giving them? Impossible to say!

If you're a cat lover, though, then you know that great moment—when you're scritching your cat behind the ears or under the chin, and then your cat leans his head with more and more weight into your palm, his eyes completely closed, a look of utter bliss etched on his face, and you not only hear but actually *feel* the rumbling sound of his purr as it ripples across the flesh of your hand...

PAWSOME!

When it's like your cat can read your mind

O kay, so mind-reading isn't really a real thing, much less a technique your kitty has actually mastered (preternaturally bright though he may be). You will almost certainly never go to the fortune-telling booth at a county fair and find a cat in full turban, sitting behind a crystal ball among billowing clouds of incense, ready to tell you the future. (*I see a white cat in your life...I see you giving him a can of tuna when you get home...*)

Even so, you'd be hard-pressed to find a cat lover who wouldn't swear up and down that cats have a knack for knowing when their humans are feeling blue and need some extra cuddling, or feeling a bit irritated and in need of some alone time, or simply in the mood to snuggle up under the covers with an old movie and a warm, purring feline for company.

And that's not even counting the way cats seem to know, some-how, the difference between when you're taking out the can open-er for a can of soup versus a can of tuna (*tuna!!!*). I'll walk back and forth across the living room a dozen times without my cats so much as batting an eyelash—but when I get up the thirteenth time, planning to "surprise" them with a treat from the Greenies bag, somehow they've already beaten me to the drawer in the end table where the Greenies are kept.

First things first, cats actually *do* have some legit superpowers: a cat's sense of smell is about fourteen times stronger than a human's, they can hear sounds three times higher than what a human can hear, and their vision (particularly at night) is far superior to ours. Not to mention that cats are basically *purr*fectly designed predators, which gives them extraordinary observation skills. You may not realize that you have your gaze turned slightly in the direction of the treats drawer when you're heading over to it—or that the cabinet holding your cans of tuna sounds *juuuuuuust* slightly different when it's opened than the cabinet where you keep your soup—but these are the kinds of things your cats will definitely make note of.

And, of course, if you're feeling sad, or anxious, or giddy and ebullient, or if you're off your usual game in some other significant way, there will be all kinds of subtle changes in the way you sit, the way you hold your body, the timbre of your voice, the size of your pupils—even, according to some studies, in the way you smell. All these nearly imperceptible things (imperceptible to humans, that is) combine to give your perceptive puss a pretty accurate gauge of what your state of mind is at any given moment.

Not that any of this explains the incredible empathy your cat is capable of on those days when you do need that extra round of purrs and cuddles to keep you going.

That's just his special gift—because your cat is
PAWSOME.

When your cat mushes his little face right up against yours

There you are, reading a book, oblivious to whatever is going on around you, when your cat approaches silently on little padded paws and doesn't just give you a "what's up?" head bonk, but actually presses his entire face to your forehead in the feline equivalent of a warm, spontaneous hug.

Or maybe you're nose to nose with him, gently scratching him behind the ears, when—after touching his nose lightly to yours—he mushes his face against your face and holds it there for a moment.

Sure, there's some "scent marking" involved here. But I think it's more than that. Cats don't have many of the same affectionate gestures at their disposal that we have at ours, after all. They can't pick us up or cuddle us in *their* laps or scritch us behind *our* ears or open a cabinet to dispense some much-loved treat to us. (Insofar as some cats *can* open cabinets and dispense treats, they typically only do so for themselves.)

But one thing your cat absolutely can do is press his face to yours and hold it there for a long moment, as if to say, *You know I love you more than anyone else in the whole world, right?*

And it's one of the greatest moments of **PAWSOME** that cat lovers live for...

When your cat waits anxiously outside the shower for you

I can only speak for myself, of course, but I get a kick out of those times when I see one or more of my cats pacing anxiously next to the shower while I'm in there.

Whether it's because they're panicked at the thought of me—*the human who feeds them,* for god's sake!—being exposed to all that water (to be trapped in an enclosed space, unable to escape the cascade of water that pours down on you relentlessly, is the stuff of kitty night terrors); or simply because I've gone to just about the only place in the house where they can't follow, I'll never know.

The one thing that's clear is that they do not like it. At. All.

Generally I'm the one worrying about the health, happiness, and wellbeing of my cats, rather than the other way around. But, still...knowing that they love me enough to worry about *my* health and wellbeing sometimes?

There's no denying...it's pretty **PAWSOME!**

When, immediately upon seeing you, your cat's tail stands straight up and vibrates

When was the last time you saw a person whom you see every single day, and they burst out with an exuberant, "OH MY GOD!!! I'M SOOOOOOO THRILLED TO SEE YOU!!!" Because that's exactly what your cat is saying when his tail sticks straight up in the air and vibrates.

And it's *the best*.

To those uninitiated into the mysteries of feline communication, it all seems simple: Dogs' tails wag when they're happy, cats' tails wag when they're *un*happy, and that's all there is to know.

But, like strangers in a strange land who will never grasp more than the rudiments of a foreign language, there's a whole lot of nuance that such people are missing out on. Cats' tails are finely tuned communication devices, able to convey a full range of moods and sentiments of which "happy" and "unhappy" are barely the tip of the iceberg.

A tail that's curved like a question mark, for example, means that it's time for you to dig out Da Bird or a favorite catnip toy, because your cat is in a playful mood. If his tail is swishing slowly from side to side, he's concentrating on something intently (possibly contemplating the best and most efficient way to persuade you to spontaneously crack open that bag of treats). When your cat gently curls his tail around you—or another cat—that's basically the equivalent of a person slinging an arm over your shoulders in a warm half-hug and saying, *Hello, friend.*

A whipping tail means that something is bothering your cat mightily and is a definite sign to any observer that backing up a foot or two (or five) is probably a wise move. A low-hanging tail can also be a sign of aggression, and a puffed-up tail like a bottle brush means that your cat is trying to look bigger than his actual size and indicates Aggression with a capital "A." (It may seem as if cats have a *lot* of ways of expressing aggression—but, considering how many times I've heard someone say, *I was just petting him and he bit me out of nowhere!* maybe they need a few more.)

But when a cat's tail sticks straight up, that means he's happy. And when his tail sticks straight up and *vibrates*—that, my feline-loving friend, is a veritable love song of enthusiasm. That's your cat's way of saying: *I love you, love you, LOVE you!!!*

We all have a tendency to take for granted the people we see every day—even the people we love the most. We don't always act as happy—or remember even to *feel* as happy—as we should when our eyes happen to fall on a beloved face. And the people who love us the most in return don't necessarily light up every time we walk into a room—especially when we've spent the last decade or two walking in and out of the exact same room to see and be seen by the exact same face.

But when your cat's tail stands straight up and does its happy dance, that's when you know there's at least one soul in this whole wide world who's downright *ecstatic* at the knowledge that a) you exist, and b) you're right here, right now, where he can gaze upon you in all your glory.

And it doesn't get any more **PAWSOME** than that.

When your cat falls asleep in your lap

L et's agree that, of all God's creatures large and small whom we humans have domesticated or been domesticated by over the millennia of our existence here on planet Earth—the dog, the horse, the bunny, to name but a few—the housecat is the most consistently and perfectly lap-sized of them all. It's the rare adult cat who's *so* small as to slip right through your lap the way a ferret would, for example. And even a full-grown Maine Coon will come much, *much* closer to fitting snugly within lap-sized confines than, say, a Great Dane.

Let's also agree that, among the numerous transcendent pleasures that come as part and parcel of living with a cat, among the most transcendent of them all is when your cat falls asleep in your lap.

Is there any greater bliss?

First and foremost, cats just look so darn *good* when they're sleeping. Maybe your cat likes to curl up in a tight ball with her tail wrapped snugly around her little nose. Maybe she sprawls out on her side, or (even better!) on her *back* with all four paws in the air, her temptingly squeezable tummy on full display. Perhaps she tucks her paws beneath her in a classic "cat as loaf of bread" pose. Whatever the sleeping position *du jour* happens to be, nothing will ever beat a lap-side view of the proceedings—an up-close and *purr*sonal perspective from which you can even see the gentle, back-and-forth sway of your kitty's whiskers as she breathes in and out.

And then there's the incomparable joy of having a semi-wild creature trust you enough to fall asleep in your lap. No cat is ever more than partially tamed at best, and cats have probably domesticated *us* at least as much as we've domesticated them. And so, in addition to the warmth and comfort all that physical closeness brings, there's also an undeniable hint of glamor—a whisper of mystery—when your cat steals softly across your legs. Nothing will ever make you feel more *chosen*. You've been selected and set apart from the great masses of humanity because of some exceptional quality you possess—a quality that's perfectly visible to your cat, even if not to yourself.

It's a moment of grace. Almost as if some wild creature had crept out of the jungle to lay his head in your lap, or some exotic bird of paradise had descended from the heavens for a fleeting moment and gently kissed you on the cheek.

If you're anything like me, the feeling of utter peace that settles over you when your cat curls or sprawls across your lap is of a deeper and more durable register than anything a paid expert in relaxation exercises or guided meditation could ever help you achieve.

Which makes it completely unsurprising that people who live with cats are forty percent less likely to suffer from heart attacks or other stress-related illnesses.

PAWSOME!

When your cat's whiskers tickle your face

A cat's whiskers are just about the cattiest cat thing going. While lots of other animals have them, we typically associate whiskers with cats—in fact, we call catfish "catfish" specifically because they, like cats, have whiskers. (Although technically what catfish have are called "barbels.")

I love seeing the profusion of my cats' whiskers—the super-long lengths of my chubbier kitty's set (whiskers typically grow out a tad wider than a cat's body, so, in the case of my husky boy, they have a lot of ground to cover!) and the more delicate span of my slender cat's. I love the abundance of them, sprouting from my cats' cheeks and above their eyes like the scraggly eyebrows and bushy beard of a very wise old man. I love watching my cats contentedly clean their whiskers following a meal, and the way they turn a shimmering, iridescent silver in the sun.

Best of all, though, is when I'm lying in bed or on the couch with my eyes closed and my cat decides to join me—and a millisecond or two before I feel the warmth of his body or the softness of his fur, I'll feel the shivery tickle of his whiskers brushing against my cheek, like wispy little heralds sent ahead to announce their master's imminent arrival.

And, in that millisecond, I know that purrs and cuddles are in my very near future.

PAWSOME!

When you fall asleep to the sound of your cat's purr

I t's something every cat has, although no two are ever exactly alike. It has magical healing properties—including the ability to promote bone growth and repair and to reduce high blood pressure. We associate it with cats, although it's a trait they share with hyenas, mongooses, raccoons, guinea pigs, genets, and civets. And even though you can't actually see it, it's something every cat lover would recognize anywhere—even in the dark.

I'm speaking, of course, about a cat's purr.

Of all the varied and glorious things there are to love about cats (I say this as someone who's compiled a whole book about them!), the purr is one of my absolute favorite things of all—and I'm guessing the same is true for you. For one thing, there are so few sounds in life that also bring with them such a pleasurable tactile *feeling* as a cat's purr. (I guess, technically, I can also feel it when my neighbor's got the bass on his stereo cranked up way too loud—but I wouldn't actually call that "pleasurable.")

And while it's true that cats will sometimes purr to "self soothe" during times of stress, it's a sound most often associated with *purr*-fect satisfaction. When you're the one causing your cat's bliss—by the well-timed application of a back scratch or ear rub, for example—hearing and feeling that deep rumble of *purr* happiness emanate from your contented kitty is the best of all possible rewards.

I love hearing my cats' purrs first thing in the morning when we've all just woken up. I love hearing purrs when I stoop to give my cats a quick scritch upon returning home after several hours away. I love hearing them as my cats are digging into their breakfast. I love it when I'm watching TV or reading a book with a cat curled up in my lap or right next to me on the couch, snoozing and purring as I stroke their back without even thinking about it.

There's never a bad time to hear the happy purrs of a happy cat, and no good thing that a good loud purr couldn't make just a wee bit better. Still, my absolute favorite of all favorite times to hear my cats' purrs is in bed at night as I'm falling asleep with one (or more!) or them right next to me. I love falling asleep to the sound of my cats' purrs more than I love falling asleep to the sounds of my favorite classical music, or a white noise machine, or the sounds of waves crashing on the shore during a beach vacation.

I think I even love falling asleep to the sound of my cats' purrs more than (don't tell him I said this!) the sound of my husband breathing next to me.

Don't get me wrong—I *love* falling asleep with my husband next to me! But, even at its deepest and most soothing, my husband's breathing doesn't have that same deep, soothing, **PAWSOME** rumble that my cats' purrs do...

Why Ask Why?

*Cats are **PAWSOME!** because...*

Cats are insanely adorable

I t's a fact so obvious that it almost goes without saying—but this book couldn't possibly be complete if it weren't stated at least once, clearly and for the record.

Your cat is adorable.

Seriously. Like, *insanely* adorable.

Those little paws, that tiny nose, those great big eyes...

And that belly! That glorious, fluffy, mushy little kitty belly!

It's enough to drive an otherwise sane and sober adult to helpless, babbling lunacy.

PAWSOME!

Cats' ears tell you how they're feeling

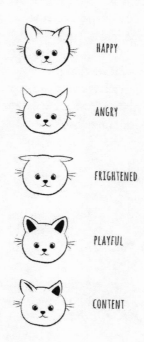

HAPPY

ANGRY

FRIGHTENED

PLAYFUL

CONTENT

PAWSOME!

Cats don't care about math

True story: I was just about finished with this book, and was getting ready to put it to bed, as we say in the biz, when—upon doing my final sweep for errors—I realized something awful:

I'd only written 100 entries; and, of course, this book's subtitle has promised *you*, dear reader, 101.

Fortunately, I had quite a few backups—there being far, *far* more than a mere 101 things to love about cats. As I was reading through them, though, trying to figure out which would be my last-minute addition, it occurred to me that one of the very best things about cats is that they would surely agree, if they could be made to understand the question, that math is basically a stupid waste of time anyway—unless you're a) an accountant, b) a literal rocket scientist, or c) trying to figure out exactly how much you'll save at a 50% off sale.

Amirite?

It's not just that cats *can't* do math. It's that if you waved a magic wand and gave them the ability to perform complex equations, they'd still make the entirely sensible decision to spend most of their time snoozing, daydreaming, looking out the window, and chasing sunbeams across the floor.

Quibbling over the very minor difference between 100 and 101 be damned.

Although I will say that my cats do seem to have the uncanny ability to figure out when I've accidentally given one of them more Pounce treats than the other.

PAWSOME!

Loving cats makes you smarter

B right as you are, you probably already knew this.

It may seem intuitively obvious that people who love cats tend to prize certain *purr*sonality traits—traits they're also likely to exhibit themselves. Introversion, sure, but also nonconformity (has your cat ever done *anything* just because you told her to?), open-mindedness (see above), and intelligence (cats manage to cozen us into feeding them despite apparently not giving a tinker's darn for what we want *them* to do—so obviously they've got something figured out). This stands opposed to the extroversion, conformity, and obedience that dog lovers seek in their own companions.

And now there's science to prove it. A 2010 study by Bristol University in the UK found that cat owners were likelier to have college and post-graduate degrees than dog owners (or any other kind of pet owner, for that matter), and a 2014 study by Carroll University in the U.S. backs that up. The U.S. study also showed that cat owners consistently score higher on intelligence tests than dog owners.

It should come as no surprise, therefore, that loving cats aligns you with some of the best and brightest figures in history—including Abraham Lincoln, Mark Twain, all three Bronte sisters, Charles Baudelaire, Ernest Hemingway, John Lennon, T.S. Eliot, William S. Burroughs, Catherine the Great, Marlon Brando, Freddie Mercury,

Neil Gaiman, Florence Nightingale, Stephen King, Jean Cocteau, Jean Paul Sartre, and Sir Isaac Newton.

There's no disputing it: Your love of cats practically assures your status as a certifiable genius.

PAWSOME!

Cats shower you with surprise gifts just because they think you're awesome

O ne of the very great joys in life is receiving gifts. Unfortunately, gift-giving occasions come around all too infrequently—and too often with disappointing results. (Show of hands if your junk drawer contains no fewer than five gift cards entitling you to $25 worth of merchandise in some store you've never spent so much as $1 in.)

And even assuming you're one of the lucky few who can count on opening a delightful box of Just What You Wanted on Christmas or birthdays, how long has it been since someone surprised you with a thoughtful present given to commemorate nothing in particular? When was the last time somebody handed you a gift-wrapped box on a random Tuesday and said, *I'm giving you this present just because I think you rock*?

Do you have to think back more than ten years to answer that question? Or is the answer maybe, just maybe, *never*?

If you live with a cat, I'm guessing your answer is more like, *A surprise gift? Why, I got one only last week!* And that's because cats *adore* bringing their humans considerate little love tokens for no other reason than to tell us, as clearly as if they'd said it in words, *Hey, you—you're WONDERFUL.*

True, our cats will rarely bring us something we would have picked out for ourselves. Cats, after all, are working within certain insurmountable limitations, such as not having charge accounts or access to Amazon Prime delivery. Also, a cat's worldview will differ in fundamental ways from a human's, tending to veer more toward the practical. Sparkly baubles are all well and good, and certainly fun to play with if they happen to dangle temptingly off the side of a dresser. But something you can *eat*—now *that's* solid gold, baby!

Which is why your felicitous feline will considerately place a small mouse or songbird—or, in the case of my own strictly indoor cats, plastic-and-felt reproductions of same—on your pillow, instead of a diamond bracelet or silk Hermés scarf.

But it's the thought that counts, and the thought in this case contains just as much downright, true-blue love as if it really were diamonds or silk. That fake mouse or disturbingly real songbird {{*shudder*}} is your cat's way of letting you know that he was think-ing about you for no darn reason other than the fact that *you*—yes, *you*—are so indescribably marvelous that he can't help but think about you All. The. Time.

Who could put a price tag on that?

I once read somewhere that the "real" reason cats leave their humans gifts is because they think we're incompetent hunters who wouldn't be able to fend for ourselves without their help. But, with all due respect to Science, I think that's a load of hooey. Cats are smart creatures, and wicked observant, and they're perfectly capable of seeing us feed ourselves—and also feed them—and putting two and two together to conclude that, however sorry and colorless our lives might be without them, we certainly wouldn't starve.

So accept this gesture of love from your adoring kitty companion, icky though it may occasionally be, for exactly what it is: a concrete testament to the profound and timeless wonder that is *you*—the single greatest human out of all the humans on the face of the earth, in your cat's considered opinion—given for no other reason except that you're simply the kind of amazing person who deserves to be showered with gifts, nonstop.

PAWSOME!

A nd you don't even have to pay to attend their "classes."

MORNING SALUTATION

KITTEN POSE

HALF LOTUS

FULL LOTUS

PLANK

THE POUNCE

PAWSOME!

Cats turn sick-days into fun-days

T here you are—sore throat, stuffy nose, a bottle of Robitussin clutched in one clammy hand, and a trashcan overflowing with wadded up Kleenex next to the bed. Sure, you've got the day off from work, and that new Stephen King you've been wanting to dive into is waiting on the nightstand.

Still, you aren't exactly having fun.

You aren't, that is, unless you're lucky enough to share your home with a cat. Because in *that* scenario, despite being down with a head cold, you're also blissfully warm and comfortably ensconced beneath the covers with a furry buddy snoozing right beside you. You're hanging out with a four-legged *fur*iend who's practically giddy with infectious joy that you're home from work today. In the middle of the week! And even though it's well past noon, *you're still in bed!*

It's like Christmas came early!

So thrilled is your kitty with this unhoped-for bonus bed time, he won't leave your side all day—no matter how red and runny your nose gets or how loudly you cough. He'll stick around long after even the most devoted spouse has headed downstairs to get on with their own phlegm-free day.

And if you want to watch *Golden Girls* reruns for the thousandth time, just because it's the one silly thing that always makes you feel better no matter how sick you are, your cat will *totally* not make fun of your choice. In fact, his ecstatic purrs as he cuddles up next to you will add a delightful harmonic accompaniment to the comedy stylings of Betty White, et al.

Bonus benefit: Your cat's purrs vibrate at just the right frequency (between 25 and 150 Hertz) to help ease breathing difficulties and promote faster healing.

PAWSOME!

Cats are sexy

There's a reason why Catwoman is indisputably the hottest female character in the entire comic-book universe.
Just sayin'.
PAWSOME!

Cats enhance your decor

Years of watching HGTV may have given you the impression that creating a home environment that's simultaneously comfortable and elegant is the kind of thing best left to professionals and those who can afford to hire them.

Stuff and nonsense! Nothing could be further from the truth.

Nobody has more panache, more casual elegance, more of what the French call *je ne sais quoi* oozing from every pore and strand in their body, than the typical housecat. And as far as comfort goes—*beesh*, please! Has anybody ever been more successful at maintaining a near-constant air of comfort and ease than our feline friends?

Here's a thought experiment that will prove just how right I am: Picture your living room as you currently have it decorated. Now picture that exact same room—with all the same furnishings—but, this time, imagine two or three chic moggies lounging about the place.

Looks one hundred percent better already, doesn't it?

So the next time you feel like giving the homestead a bit of a spruce, there's no need to clip pictures from *Better Homes and Gardens* or go into hock at the Home Depot. Stop by your local shelter instead.

Happy home, happy cat, happy life.
PAWSOME!

Cats are excellent judges of character

In his book *Celebrating Cats*, Roger A. Caras writes: "Tradition has it that Adolf Hitler hated cats. He probably did; everything else was wrong with him."

While the point about the profound personality flaws of cat haters is well taken, I'd prefer to think that it was the other way around—that it's not so much that truly detestable people don't like cats. Rather, it's the *cats*—sensing all that detestability—who will avoid such a person at all costs.

I have absolutely no way of proving it, and sadly there aren't any scientific studies (that I'm aware of) to confirm it, but it's been my experience that cats are shrewd and insightful appraisers of human nature. My husband who, when I first met him, believed himself to be "not a cat guy," turned out to be easy pickings for my cat Vashti, who had him wrapped around her snow-white paw inside of a month by a) being gorgeous, and b) singling him out for special, affectionate attention.

(*But she's so pretty, and she likes me!* my husband would protest, whenever I chided him for feeding Vashti from the table, or giving her extra treats at night, or engaging in some other obvious act of feline vassalage.)

The point being, there was a dedicated cat lover lurking inside my husband-to-be all along. It simply took the keenly observant eye of a cat to suss it out.

Every cat I've ever met has known within nanoseconds that I'm a complete sucker, utterly unable to resist a pair of sad eyes or a pleading paw placed on my knee before I cave in and do whatever the kitty in question wants. When I was a kid, cats used to follow me on my way to school, and they'd have me dispensing the food from my lunchbox faster than a mobster shakes down the owners of a mom-and-pop grocery store.

And I've never known a single person who my cats thoroughly despised—instantly and upon meeting them—who turned out to be worth a darn.

So the next time you're wondering whether some new acquaintance is all they're cracked up to be, bring them around for your cat to size up. If they turn out to be a less-than-desirable companion, believe me your cat will know—and she'll make sure you do, too.

Nothing beats feline intuition, which is powerful and **PAWSOME!**

Zoomies!

When was the last time you ran around like a maniac for no other reason than the glory of movement itself? The ecstasy of pumping energy back into your muscles after lying down for a long time? To chase an imaginary squirrel or playmate you'd made up in your head? Just for the sheer, irrepressible *joy* of it?

Because your cat does that all the time. And it's
PAWSOME!

(Except for the not-so-pawsome 4:00 a.m. zoomies...what is *up* with that???)

Poop zoomies!

T here's no consensus opinion as to why, exactly, some cats will hightail it away from the litter box the second they're done using it as if they were fleeing a crime scene. Bashfulness? Self-consciousness? Some residual evolutionary fear of predators sniffing them out?

For the record, cats in the wild don't flee their poop. Assuming, of course, that you and your vet have ruled out any digestive issues, it seems that the four *actual* potential answers to this question are:

- Because it's hilarious

- Because cats are deeply weird

- Because your cat wants you to be aware—and appropriately admiring—of her latest...um..."accomplishment"

- Because your cat doesn't want to be standing too close to any incriminating evidence when someone in your house says, "Do you smell something *odd*?"

No matter how bad a day I'm having, "poop zoomies" (mostly perpetrated by my cat Fanny, an odd and self-conscious little sprite of a cat) will always crack me up.

And anything that generates a guaranteed laugh is, without question, **PAWSOME**!

Dat ass

I f I had a nickel for every time I've awakened first thing in the morning to find a cat bum wedged firmly against my face, I'd have a mountain of nickels stretching higher than the Matterhorn.

I'm guessing that you, dear reader, can say the same.

Cats love showing off their butts. There's the tail lift, the backside bump (when your cat, walking past you, casually bonks his hindquarters against your shin), the "elevator butt," (when you're scratching your cat's back near the base of his tail and he raises his hindquarters in response), the full-on face plant (and the aforementioned waking up nose to...er..."nose" with a feline derriere).

For sheer inventiveness in coming up with so very many ways to work their butts into the conversation, as it were, our cats deserve to be commended. *Look at it!* seems to be their constant demand. *Admire it! Behold my butt in all its terrible glory!*

Students of feline psychology will offer all sorts of scientific explanations to account for why cats are so fascinated with making sure *we're* so fascinated with their backsides. And while I'm sure that's all completely legit, let's be honest: Cats are constantly showing off their butts because they think—nay, they *know*—that their butts are worth showing off. And however much we may protest, we feel the same.

We love cat butts. We can't get enough of cat butts. We're practically cat-butt junkies.

Scoff at me all you like, but as Exhibit A I invite you to visit Amazon and do a search for "cat butt coloring books." Go ahead, I'll wait.

By the time you come back here—having made your way past dozens of pedestrian titles like "Cat Butts: A Coloring Book" and "A Cat Butt Birthday" all the way to "Cat Butts in Space: The Feline Frontier"—you'll have to concede the point. And that's before we even delve deeper (ahem) into the virtual Aladdin's Cave of cat butt swag available on the open market for the discerning ailurophile: cat butt stickers, cat butt calendars, cat butt refrigerator magnets, cat butt necklaces and earrings, cat butt wine-bottle stoppers, cat butt tissue holders (because who *wouldn't* want to pull a fresh Kleenex out of a cat's wazoo?), cat-butt-shaped shoulder bags, cat butt t-shirts and hoodies, crocheted cat butt coasters, cat butt coffee mugs...

I could go on (I really could, because all this stuff is still only the tip of the cat butt iceberg), but I feel like my point's probably been made.

My own personal theory as to why we're so oddly enamored of kitty tushes goes something like this: Cats lift their tails to show us their butts when they're particularly happy with us, and in doing so they've trained us to be particularly happy when we're "rewarded" with that upward flick.

Not to mention that there's something indisputably aesthetically pleasing about the perfectly round and puckered pimento nestled back there in our cats' nether regions, and we may as well just admit it. And who among us, upon observing the jaunty little sway of a cat's behind as she walked away, hasn't found themselves thinking, *Shake it, don't break it, baby!*

The bottom line (hee!) is that cat butts are among the consistently greatest butts out there. And if you're a person who lives with a cat, then you're lucky enough to have daily access to one in all its sassy, saucy, seein'-is-believin' splendor.

PAWSOME!

C ats have some of the most beautiful eyes in the world...

And sometimes their eyes look like lasers!

PAWSOME!

Cats are graceful.
Except when they're not.

This is a true story:

My lithe little Fanny—a delicate and fine-boned ballerina of a cat—leapt nimbly four feet up from the floor to our six-inch-wide marble mantelpiece and deftly wended her way across it, weaving among the framed photos, vases, and candlesticks without so much as grazing a single one. In one graceful bound, she then flew from the mantelpiece to the even-narrower (perhaps three inches wide) back of the sofa, and stealthily cat-walked her way from one end to the other before gently descending back down to the floor ten feet away from where she'd originally started, noiseless as a cloud in her dismount.

I'm not sure what the point of the expedition was other than, possibly, to impress the two klutzy, graceless humans who were watching her. (That would be my husband and me, and we were suitably impressed.)

The very next day, the same cat tried to leap from the floor onto our coffee table, which is a mere eighteen inches high and wide as the side of a barn. There was one—and only one—thing on that enormous coffee table, other than a few tasteful photography books: a small dish of salsa resting next to a plate of chips. Given how very large the entire landing surface of the table was, and how comparatively small the bowl of salsa, you'd almost have to be aiming right for it to hit it.

Nevertheless, that's exactly what Fanny did. Caught one paw in the bowl, which promptly flipped into the air before coming to rest (spilling its contents, naturally) on a white, faux-fur shag rug. Fanny herself didn't even stick the landing, but rather tumbled tush over teacup onto the ground, landing in a clumsy heap of fur.

Moral of the story: Cats are graceful. Except when they're not.

And that little bit of unpredictability is just one more thing that makes living with cats so very entertaining...

And so very **PAWSOME!**

"Making biscuits"

I don't know about you, but I love a knead-y cat.

Not all cats "make biscuits"—which is when a cat pushes in and out with his paws, alternating between left and right—but lots of them do. As with all things cat-centric, there's no one clear-cut answer as to why cats do this (comfort and scent-marking are two big contenders), although one thing's for sure: If a kitty's kneading on you, it's an unmistakable sign of affection and contentment.

My cat Clayton adores kneading on soft things, like our mushiest pillows. His other favorite thing to "make biscuits" on is the roll of flesh just above the waistband of my jeans. Which I guess means that my belly and our mushiest pillows are (from Clayton's perspective, anyway) of a similar texture and consistency. Which *definitely* means I'll be demanding a refund on my Abs Roller, posthaste.

PAWSOME!

Cats are perfect miniature
space heaters

B ack in the Olden-Time Days of Yore (an official term I just
made up), before the advent of central heating, figuring out
the best way to heat a bed on a cold winter's night was a devilishly
tricky conundrum.

In the Middle Ages, a servant might heat a brick or large rock in
the fireplace and then rub it on the bedsheets—although warming
your sheets with a rock, only to have them get cold again ten minutes
later, was probably even less fun than it sounds. Fancy metal bed
warmers, which replaced heated bricks, worked roughly the same
way (fill them with hot embers, rub them all over the sheets) and,
again, produced temporary-at-best results, along with the constant
danger of scorching the bed linens. Hot-water bottles eventually
came along to replace bed warmers, but they were made of rubber
and apt to wear thin eventually or just plain wear out—not to mention that you'd inevitably (and rather unpleasantly) wake up the next
morning to find a *cold* rubber bottle of water in bed with you.

Yuck, yuck, and *yuck*.

This is a prime example of humans working awfully hard to solve
a problem that nature already solved for us a long time ago. Your
trusty feline's normal body temperature runs just a scooch above
yours (in the 99.5 to 102.5 degree range) and isn't prone to cooling
overnight—like, say, that rubber water bottle is. Plus, cats are just
the right size to fit snugly under the covers without taking up more

space than is comfortable for the sprawl of your own arms and legs. So having a deliciously warm and furry friend cuddled deep beneath the blankets with you, by your feet or at your side, is an excellent way to stave off the cold when the thermometer plunges.

And if you can work it out so that you have two or three or even *four* cats to pile into bed with you (literally—it's best when they all just pile right on top of you), then you'll be in an enviable position, indeed. I'm talking about a blissful purr-puddle of body heat—albeit one that will make it excruciatingly difficult for you to get out of bed the following day. (Is there anything better than cuddling in bed with your kitties on a frosty winter morning?)

On the other hand, those warm and cozy overnight hours will be deeply sublime.

Confession: Sometimes in the winter, when I'm writing at the desk in my home office—wearing socks but no shoes, naturally enough—I'll move one of the cats' beds so that it's directly below my feet, thus tempting said cat to curl up curl up close enough to my toes (or even directly on top of my toes) to keep them comfy and warm, no matter how bone-chillingly cold it gets outside.

Toasty toes all January long? **PAWSOME!**

Cats can operate NASA spacecraft

I swear it's true.

Well...it's sort of true.

Daniel Lakey is a NASA spacecraft-operations engineer who works on the European Space Agency's Solar Orbiter, an unmanned spacecraft that circles the sun and sends back all kinds of information to scientists here on Earth.

Like just about everybody else with an office job, Lakey was ordered to work from home during the Covid-19 crisis—where, as reported to *The Atlantic*, he was subjected to the not-so-tender mercies and constant interference of his two feline housemates, Sparkle and Buttons.

Sparkle, in particular, was fond of commandeering Lakey's computer keyboard—both while Lakey was at his desk performing the task of managing a solar orbiter millions of miles from Earth, and also whenever he left his computer unattended.

Of course, there are plenty of fail-safes in place to keep a cat from *actually* directing the orbital path of a NASA spacecraft. Still, cats are pretty handy with a keyboard once they've taken one over, as anyone with cats can f02g%$*#23g;jhldf!$#!

Apparently, Sparkle isn't the only NASA-affiliated feline with sky-high as*purr*ations. On April 7th, astrophysicist Amber Straughn tweeted:

Actually discussed in a virtual meeting today: how to keep cats from accidentally commanding spacecraft while this work is going on in people's homes on laptops instead of inside a cat-free NASA building. #catsofquarantine

And there you have it.

So the next time you hear a report of a UFO sighting, consider the possibility that what's been spotted overhead is a spacecraft that very much originated here on planet Earth—but that's temporarily veering wildly off course because it's fallen into the fuzzy clutches of Sparkle or Buttons, or some other furry miscreant whose human servant is a NASA employee.

Godspeed, brave space kitties of the sky! You have the right stuff, and you're absolutely **PAWSOME!**

Cats are pros at social distancing

"Social distancing" is one of those expressions you probably never heard once in your whole life until sometime circa March of 2020—and then, suddenly, you heard it *everywhere*. Constantly. All the freaking time.

In the era of Covid-19, the gist of "social distancing" is this: Stay home for the most part. Avoid crowds of more than a few people. Stand at least six feet away from anybody you don't live with.

In other words, do exactly what your cat has already been doing her entire life *by choice*.

Cats: once again ahead of the curve, leaving the rest of us racing to catch up.

Because cats are brilliant. And they're also **PAWSOME!**

Cats make the best napping buddies

A midafternoon nap—known in Spanish as a *siesta*—is possibly the most civilized custom that the entirety of Western civilization has ever produced.

Sadly, however, *siestas* aren't looked upon in a favorable light outside of Spain and Latin America. While a midday nap can make it possible to both get up earlier and stay up later—thus extending your potentially productive daily hours in both directions—and while study after study has shown that the human body tends to crave a brief nap in the 2:00 p.m. range, people who make a habit of napping in the middle of the afternoon are generally regarded as loafers. Idlers. Vagabonds and layabouts.

But napping is awesome, and nobody understands that better than your cat. In fact, nobody in the world understands *anything* better than your cat understands napping. Your cat possesses encyclopedic knowledge and *very* strong opinions on everything from ideal nap durations to best practices for choosing and maintaining a nap position, not to mention a minute understanding of the subtle pros and cons when comparing various napping surfaces (mattress versus floor versus sofa versus windowsill versus easy chair...et cetera).

So if you're looking for a partner in crime who will not only approve of your socially frowned-upon midday nap, but who will probably form the sagacious opinion that, *This may be the smartest thing I've ever seen her do*, look no further than your feline best bud.

I don't know about you, but sometimes—when I walk into the bedroom to find one or both of my cats sprawled out and snoozing across the bed in unselfconscious, luxurious bliss—I think to myself that nobody makes napping look so *good* as my cats do. And on those occasions when I indulge in my own midday *siesta*, I never nap more restfully than I do when my cats pile into bed with me, warmly purring their very strong approval of what is, in their opinion, an infinitely wise life choice that I've made.

I'm not sure why it is, but something about falling asleep with one cat leaning heavily against my leg, and the other curled up in the crook between my arm and my torso, makes me fall asleep more quickly, sleep more deeply, and wake up more refreshed than if I were going it alone. Maybe it's the warm glow of approval and acceptance I drift off to dreamland basking in, or maybe there's some actual physiological explanation to account for this.

Maybe it's both.

All I can tell you is that if you haven't tried it already, you definitely should. Those guilt-free afternoons you spend napping the nap of the just—your furry little *siesta* gurus cuddled up at your side—will be blissful, restful, and one hundred percent **PAWSOME!**

Cats are so soft...

L ike, seriously—*soooooooooooooo* soft.

The only thing softer might be a sable. But good luck getting a sable to come live in your house and purr in your lap.

A cat, however, will do just that—allowing you to sink your fingers deep into that thick, soft, luxurious fur—for very little more than the price of a litter box, some annual vet visits, and a heaping helping of lifelong, unconditional love.

PAWSOME!

KITTENS!

Kittens! Kittens! Kittens! Kittens! Kittens! Kittens! Kittens! Kittens!
Kittens! Kittens! Kittens! Kittens! Kittens! Kittens! Kittens! Kittens!
Kittens! Kittens! Kittens! Kittens! Kittens! Kittens! Kittens! Kittens!
Kittens! Kittens! Kittens! Kittens! Kittens! Kittens! Kittens! Kittens!
Kittens! Kittens! Kittens! Kittens! Kittens! Kittens! Kittens! Kittens!
Kittens! Kittens! Kittens! Kittens! Kittens! Kittens! Kittens! Kittens!
Kittens! Kittens! Kittens! Kittens! Kittens! Kittens! Kittens! Kittens!
Kittens! Kittens! Kittens! Kittens! Kittens! Kittens! Kittens! Kittens!
Kittens! Kittens! Kittens! Kittens! Kittens! Kittens! Kittens! Kittens!
Kittens! Kittens! Kittens! Kittens! Kittens! Kittens! Kittens! Kittens!
Kittens! Kittens! Kittens! Kittens! Kittens! Kittens! Kittens! Kittens!
Kittens! Kittens! Kittens! Kittens! Kittens! Kittens! Kittens! Kittens!
Kittens! Kittens! Kittens! Kittens! Kittens! Kittens! Kittens! Kittens!
Kittens! Kittens! Kittens! Kittens! Kittens! Kittens! Kittens! Kittens!
Kittens! Kittens! Kittens! Kittens! Kittens! Kittens! Kittens! Kittens!

PAWSOME!

Cats are natural musicians

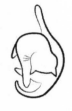

They play the cello.

They sing for their supper.

Sometimes they even play the piano!

Keyboard Cat

PAWSOME!

Cats aren't afraid to be alone with their thoughts

Once upon a time, it was taken for granted that there would be certain idle moments in the day—waiting at a stoplight, standing in line at a deli counter—when you would be alone with your thoughts. When there'd be nothing for you to focus on for entire minutes at a time other than your own inner monologue and whatever haphazard ideas might be bobbing along in your stream of consciousness.

But the beeping, buzzing, ubiquitous presence of smartphones seems to have filled up all those "empty" moments in the day and pretty much guaranteed that none of us is ever alone anymore in any truly meaningful sense, much less alone with our thoughts. And while I'm all for maintaining human contact, I sometimes wonder if we've become *afraid* of what we might find rattling around in our heads if we spent a few minutes every day and really looked.

Cats, on the other hand, *adore* being alone with their thoughts and never seem to worry about what they might find germinating in the deep dark recesses of their feline psyches. Looking thoughtfully out of a window or straight ahead into empty space is one of your cat's favorite ways to pass the time, when she isn't sleeping. And while it's impossible to know precisely what's running through a cat's mind at any given moment, who—upon seeing the contemplative expression in those mysterious, Sphinx-like eyes—could doubt that it's something infinitely fascinating and wise?

Okay, so maybe what your cat is *actually* thinking is more along the lines of, *I'd love to murder that bird on the windowsill...* But, still! At least cats aren't freaked out by their own murderous impulses.

The Buddha once said that the path to Enlightenment begins with learning how to think, how to wait, and how to fast. And while I'm one hundred percent confident that no cat will ever master the whole fasting thing, cats' superior skills when it comes to waiting and thinking clearly mean they're farther down that Enlightenment path than we are.

In which case, we can only benefit from having their **PAWSOME** example shining before us!

Cats remind us that being curious and being persistent are two great ways to go through life

S top me if this sounds familiar: While you're generally happy to share just about everything in your life and your home with your cat, there's *one* thing in your house—one shelf, one cabinet, one big box of holiday goodies—that you'd prefer Patches kept her fuzzy little paws away from.

And naturally, cats being the perverse creatures they are, that's the precise shelf, cabinet, and/or box that Patches finds completely irresistible.

I remember a few years back, when a reader sent me a huge carton filled with those miniature felt-covered toy mice for me to distribute at some of the cat shelters where I do readings. My black cat Fanny—a lithe little imp if ever there was one—*adores* those miniature toy mice. Fanny also makes a determined point of sticking her nose into every box, bag, and parcel that finds its way into our house, believing (not entirely without reason) that, in doing so, she's apt to discover things she'd probably enjoy, but that I would be unlikely to share with her. Sensing disaster as soon as I opened one flap of this cardboard box of and saw what was inside, I therefore bundled it way into a back corner of our rarely used guest-room closet.

But, of course, my attempt at keeping it hidden from the keenly observant and fiendishly clever Fanny was doomed from the start. About a week later, I came home to a bonanza of tiny felt-covered toy mice strewn across the guest bedroom, the main bedroom, and the living room.

That was the day when I spent over one hundred dollars to replace a bunch of tiny toy mice, and the day when Fanny got a hundred brand-new toy mice all at one time.

The moral of the story—at least from Fanny's perspective—is that curiosity and persistence pay off.

There's a certain kind of person who's fond of quoting the old adage, *Curiosity killed the cat.* Such people only get away with their party-poopery, however, by conveniently lopping off the second half of that saying, which tells us, *But satisfaction brought him back.*

Being consistently curious is a wonderful way to go through life. Curious people learn more things and know more things. They're better conversationalists, and they're constantly engaged with the world. Curiosity is one of those habits of mind that will keep your mind young long past the point when it's gotten difficult—if not impossible—to keep your body in the same condition.

And as a bona fide bestselling author who's nevertheless racked up more than twenty rejections for every one acceptance I've ever gotten, I can attest from hard-won experience that persistence, in this life, is everything.

Cats are born knowing this already.

So the next time you find yourself sighing with exasperation over a handful of Q-tips (now repurposed as ad hoc cat toys) that your frisky feline discovered on a bathroom shelf during one of his daily reconnaissance missions, remember not to be *too* irritated.

Think of your cat as a live-in life coach, guiding you through the intricacies of making the most of your time on this earth. There are, after all, foolish rich people who pay thousands of dollars to actual human life coaches in exchange for a service that *you* are getting entirely for free, from your very own cat.

PAWSOME!

Cats are easy to entertain

Maybe you think of yourself as the life of the party. Or, maybe you struggle to overcome the sense that you're the dull party guest who the other guests wish they hadn't gotten stuck talking to on their way to the bar.

If you're like most of us, you probably toggle somewhere between those two polarities, landing closer to one end of the spectrum or the other depending on your mood, what kind of hair day you're having, or how many new and interesting anecdotes you've shored up since the last time everyone got together.

This is one among thousands of reasons why spending time with cats is so, *so* great—because cats are just about the easiest audience ever. Smart as they are, it's nevertheless almost ridiculously simple to entertain a cat. A laser pointer will do the job, or a bottle cap, or an errant feather from a pillow wafting in the air. You could attach a bird feeder to one of your windows, and—presto! Instant Cat TV!

Heck, you could even tie a cotton ball to a piece of string, and staple that string to a stick you found in your yard, and your cat would be all like, *OMG THIS IS GENIUS!!!!!!!!!!!!!!!!!*

In short, nobody will ever make you feel like a more fascinating and naturally gifted entertainer than your cat will. And to paraphrase another legendary entertainer, the late great Jackie Gleason:

"How **PAWSOME** it is!"

Cats shred toilet paper, tissues, and paper towels

On the downside, it can be rather vexing to have little Jinxie blithely lay waste to so many paper goods when the price of *everything* is going up and up—and when it's not like she's going to stick around to help you clean up the mess she's just made.

On the upside, though, it kinda looks as if a super-festive ticker-tape parade has just passed through your house.

You can even pretend the parade was thrown for you, just 'cause you're so **PAWSOME**!

Cats knock things off of tables and shelves

H ear me out!

Yes, I *totally* understand how this might actually seem like one of the (very few) *annoying* things about living with cats. Sure, it's hilarious when you're watching a video of *somebody else's* cat knocking glassware or pottery off a kitchen counter. That isn't your problem, after all. You can afford to chuckle at *that* person's expense as you cast a smug look over at your own Shadow or Snowball, adorably curled up on the couch—sleeping so angelically that you can practically see a little halo floating above her head.

It's decidedly less funny, however, when the object that's going down is one that's in your very own house—when the cat in question is *your* cat, and what's being destroyed is one of the set of long-stemmed, hand-blown champagne glasses that you wrapped in a dozen newspapers and carefully packed in five soft t-shirts before carrying them all the way back from your vacation in Stockholm (true story); or the photo of your great-grandparents' wedding, framed in irreplaceable antique glass and bequeathed to you by your grandmother (also a true story); or the unattended glass of water you left on the coffee table for *two seconds*, only to see your cat swipe it down onto the hardwood floor FOR ABSOLUTELY NO REASON—LIKE, SERIOUSLY, *NO REASON AT ALL!*—and *now* you have to spend the next half-hour crawling around on your hands and knees with a flashlight so you can make super-extra-one-hundred-percent sure it hasn't left behind any tiny little shards you might have missed, and that will *definitely* find their way into a hapless foot or feline paw if they remain undiscovered. (Like pulling a thousand glass splinters out of your own foot wouldn't *still* be better than having to delve into your cat's paw with a pair of tweezers and a tube of antiseptic ointment...)

Ahem.

I feel your pain, is what I'm saying. But consider this: How many times, over the years, have you unwrapped a wedding/housewarming/graduation/hostess gift, only to discover some truly heinous—some genuinely hideous and godawful monstrous—vase/pitcher/picture frame/what-have-you, that you not only have to demonstrate gratitude for ("I've always wanted a set of drinking glasses with Pamela Anderson's face on them!"), but that you're actually expected to *display* in some prominent place? ("These are going right on the bar cart where everybody can see them!")

Sure, you can discreetly pack them back up and stick them high on some unreachable closet shelf as soon as the gift-giver departs. Don't think for a minute, though, that said gift-giver won't notice the items are missing the next time they come over to your house. ("Hey—what happened to those Pam Anderson glasses I got you?")

If you live with a cat, however, you have an easy and obvious way out. "You know how Tiger is," you'll be able to reply, casting your eyes down with just the right amount of feigned disappointment. "She knocked them clean off the bar cart, and they shattered into little bits." And then, with a despondent sigh, you can add, "She's a stinker, all right, but what can you do?"

Problem solved!

The best part is that your cat—who, let's face it, is ENTIRELY unrepentant even when she destroys something that you actually do love—won't mind at all if you pin the blame on her. She won't lose one single second of sleep, out of the roughly fifty-seven thousand seconds she spends sleeping every day, for worrying about it.

Having a fuzzy little love bug who lives in your house and plies you with purrs? That's amazing.

Having a partner in crime who's willing to take all the blame and provide you with an airtight alibi?

That's **PAWSOME!**

Cats are experts at getting comfortable

A nd they always make snoozing look sooooooo good...

PAWSOME!

Cats heroically sacrifice themselves to protect you from bad news

S ometimes you don't even know the grenade is there until someone else bravely throws themselves on top of it just to save you.

Case in point, the newspaper I intended to open the other morning. Just as I was about to peruse Page One headlines blaring their
end-times updates of plague, pestilence, and economic carnage,
however, my cat Fanny ran at a gallop from clear across the room,
took a nimble flying leap high into the air, and landed smack in the
middle of the newspaper. She then flopped onto her side and flung
out all four of her legs—so as to achieve maximum sprawl—before
rolling adorably onto her back.

She was so very adorable, in fact, that the irresistible,
weapons-grade force of her adorableness reduced me to a simpleton,
babbling helplessly in her direction (*Who's a silly girl? Who's my
silly, silly girl?*), while my gallant Fanny—with no concern for what
effects the day's dreadful news might have on *her*—flopped back
onto her stomach and began happily clawing up the paper beneath
her, effectively shredding it to bits and thus sparing me from an
unbearably depressing morning.

It was a close call.

In households all over the world, every single day, this same ritual
of self-sacrifice is repeated by fearless felines of all description. Cats
both old and young, slim and portly, aloof and clingy, hyperac-
tive and brazenly lazy, are bravely shielding their beloved human

companions—*using their own bodies!*— from any incursion by the horrors contained in innocent-looking daily newspapers.

Most of us, while we're either sighing in frustration over our pilfered paper (*Bad kitty! That's* mommy's *newspaper!*) or affectionately rubbing the ears of the cat perched atop it, will never know just how close a brush with disaster we had.

Everyone loves to talk about the altruism of dogs. But dogs make such a big *show* of guarding their humans—forever barking and growling and jumping, and generally making such a spectacle of themselves—that *of course* you're basically *forced* to commend their protectiveness. (Even when they're "protecting" you from perfectly helpful people, like the mail carrier or the delivery driver with your takeout chicken, which is a mistake your cat will never make.)

True heroes toil in the shadows, where their heroism is generally misunderstood or overlooked altogether. But know, beloved feline companions, that some of us are aware how very deep your sacrifice goes.

And, to us, you will always remain the very embodiment of **PAWSOME**!

Cats like to catch bugs

D o you like catching bugs in *your* house?

I don't like catching bugs in *my* house.

Fortunately for all of us, cats love catching bugs! Nothing makes a cat's day like the opportunity to dismember a cockroach, dispatch a housefly, or tackle the horror-movie-sized spider that's terrorizing you in the bathroom. A task so thoroughly unpleasant as to constitute a mild form of mental torture (to squish, or not to squish? <<shudder>>) is the equivalent of a three-day holiday weekend kicked off by concerts and fireworks, as far as your cat is concerned.

Best of all, your wily feline will almost always get her man...er...bug.

Less expensive than hiring a professional exterminator and way, *way* cuter.

PAWSOME!

Cats go perfectly with books

Formula for the *purr*fect Sunday:

Sunlight in the windows, birdsong in your ears, a good thick book in your hands, and a warm, purring cat in your lap.

PAWSOME!

Raspy tongues

I f you were blindfolded and trying to pick out a cat from among a bunch of other animals, using only your sense of touch, it might not be as easy as you'd think. Soft fur wouldn't be much of a tip-off, for example—just about every mammal, especially the domesticated ones who share our homes with us, have fur. Tails are also pretty ubiquitous. Same goes for claws and sharp teeth. Running your hand over a snout-full of whiskers wouldn't be much of a help; cats have whiskers in common with dogs, ferrets, rats, gerbils, horses, and even seals and walruses.

But there's nothing quite so distinct, so *paw*sitively and unmistakably feline, as a cat's raspy tongue. In fact, to have felt a cat's raspy tongue along your arm even once is to be able to pick out the raspy tongue of any cat anywhere—even while blindfolded.

The reason why feline tongues have their trademark rasp is because they're covered in a type of hooked, hollow bristle called *filiform papillae*. You've probably already heard that these bristles help cats clean and detangle their fur during the grooming process. The barbs on cats' tongues also help them to rasp the meat from the bones of their prey.

That's why raspy tongues are good for our cats. They're good for *us*, however, simply because they're…well…because they're so *raspy*. It might seem contradictory to describe a feeling as being both "rough" and also "affectionate," and yet what two words better apply to the sandpapery sensation of being lovingly "groomed" by your cat?

Being licked by his own mama cat when he was a kitten is the first tactile memory that any cat has. His mom would have licked him clean immediately after he was born, and used her tongue as a combination washcloth and scent marker all over the kitten's coat, ears, and every part of his tiny body when he was still very small. So when your cat includes you now in this deeply ingrained ritual of love, it's hard to imagine a higher compliment.

(Just so long as your cat doesn't "compliment" you for too long. Remember: those barbed tongues were designed to strip the meat off of bones!)

It's very sweet when a dog enthusiastically licks you, but dogs' tongues have a *slight* tendency to be just a *wee* bit spit-riddled and (sorry!) even slimy—two sins that your cat's tongue will almost certainly never commit.

And that, once again, is because cats' tongues are just so, *so* raspy. **PAWSOME!**

Cats will warm your favorite chair for you

I haven't had to sit in a cold chair or climb into a chilly bed since 1995.

That was the year when I first started living with cats.

I've seen my cats devote hours—heck, I've seen them devote entire *days*—to thoughtfully warming up my favorite easy chairs, sofa cushions, and bed pillows for me. Sometimes they'll sacrifice so many of their own leisure hours to ensuring my comfort that I have to *beg* them to stop, to plead with them that it really is okay, that they've warmed up the recliner sufficiently to protect my posterior from any possible contact with a less-than-toasty surface, and that all I want now is to relax and watch whatever new version of *The Great British Bake Off* Netflix is promoting these days.

Still, it can take as long as a full half-hour of imploring (sometimes I have to implore at the top of my lungs) before I'm finally able to persuade my conscientious kitties that they've done enough to help me for one day and can get up now. (*Seriously, guys—get up now!*)

That's how devoted to me my cats are.

It's a kind of dedication to service—a selflessness, really—that on doesn't encounter very often these days.

But when you do, and especially when it's being demonstrated by your very own cats, it's a **PAWSOME** thing to behold!

Cats know how to throw shade

D o you ever think your problem is that you're just too *nice*? Do you sometimes wish you knew how to crush people into insignificance with a single, withering gaze?

Good news: your cat is here to help! When it comes to throwing a single scornful glance—the kind that doesn't necessarily make you feel invisible, but kinda makes you wish you were—nobody can hold a candle to your supercilious and somewhat snobbish feline. With a single disdainful sniff, or one cool glance before turning her head away, your cat, when she wants to, is very eloquently able to convey the message: *Leave me now, worm.*

Your mileage may vary, but suffice it to say that when I've had guests in my home over the years who one or more of my cats didn't care for, nobody was ever in any doubt as to how the cats felt. In particular, my surly girl Scarlett—who never met a stranger she had the smallest particle of use for—had a way of turning her backside, flicking her tail dismissively, and stalking coldly away that might have abashed Queen Elizabeth herself, had the Queen for some reason found herself of an afternoon taking tea in our Midtown Manhattan high-rise.

(Good god, I miss that cat so much!)

My point isn't that cats are actually the mean-spirited creatures naysayers try to make them out to be. But those naysayers tend to be the kind of people who don't like cats—and who cats therefore, in their infinite wisdom, show their colder side to—and that kind of *is* the point.

In short: Don't waste time on the haters. Give them the haughty side-eye and move on with your day.

You'll be glad your **PAWSOME** cat showed you how!

Naming a cat is super fun!

*C*ats the musical has divided the opinions of theater aficionados since long before its big-screen adaptation became a conspicuous flop. But even the most jaded theatergoer would have to concede that the names of *Cats'* feline characters may be the most entertaining roster in theater history: Bustopher Jones, Jennyanydots, Skimbleshanks, Rum Tum Tugger, Bombalurina, Rumpleteazer, Mister Mistoffelees, and Grindlebone, to name just a few.

We can't all have a gift for wordplay like the great poet T.S. Eliot, author of the delightful *Old Possum's Book of Practical Cats*, upon which *Cats* is based. Still, each time we adopt a cat, we have the opportunity to let our imaginations roam free—to go beyond Socks, Smoky, Mittens, or Midnight and flex our creative muscles.

I, myself, have been the proud kitty custodian of Scarlett (named for her tendency to faint in her early kitten-hood), Vashti (named for the beautiful Persian queen), my blind cat Homer (an homage to the blind Greek poet), Clayton "the Tripod" (named for the one-legged tap dancer Clayton "Peg Leg" Bates), and Fanny (a family name—I had great-aunt Fannys on both sides—although my UK readers are forever reminding me of its less-innocent connotations).

While writing this book, I asked my readers to contribute the names of their own cats, as well as the best and worst cat names they'd ever heard. Here's an entirely unscientific sampling of the results:

The Good:

Bobaloo, Earl Grey, Oliver, Kerfuffle, Blackula, Paw McCatney, Penelope, Momo, Rigatoni, Casper, Herman, Vixen, Thumbelina, Boris and Natasha, Death and Taxes (two black cats), Pickles, Maggie, Tumbleweed, Oscar, John Henry, Jim Morrison, Ziggy, Nico, Sabrina, Max, Hermes, Jojo, Chairman Meow, Gypsy Rose, Bubbles, Peanut, Trixie, Fonzie, Hendrix, Hercules, Lancelot, Houdini, Figaro, Gus, Frida Cat-lo, and Noodles

The Bad:

Dog, Dawg, Bluecifer, Baby Jesus, Darth Kitty, Puss, Natas (Satan spelled backward), Cat, Other Cat, Smelly Cat, Cutie Patootie, Chicken Nugget, Fatness Neverclean (presumably a riff on Katniss Everdeen from the *Hunger Games* books), Fluffy Fusty Feather Fungus, Dot Com, Mocha Latte, Fruity Pebbles, Peepants, Gus 2, Final Gus, and Gus 4: The Re-Gus-ening

The Ugly:

Sh-thead (this was BY FAR the most common response I got when I asked for the worst cat names my readers had ever heard), Penis Face, Hitler, Adolf, Crackhead, Bimbo, Stinky, Stinkus, Mud Butt, Mieskeit (literally Yiddish for "ugly"), Booger, Snot, Scabies, Garbage, Chemo, Mucous, and Spit

Sometimes cats are made of liquid

PAWSOME!

Cats are self-cleaning

Things in your life that you have to clean:

Your floors
Your dishes
Your refrigerator
Your toilet
Your bathtub
Your books, bookcases, CDs, picture frames, and assorted knick-knacks
Your clothes
Your kitchen counters
Your toddler
Your dog

Things in your life that are self-cleaning:

Your cat
Maybe your oven?

When it comes to household chores, your cats are all about simplifying your life.
PAWSOME!

Cats hang out with you in the bathroom and never, ever judge

The great mass of humanity as a whole can't come to a uniform consensus on just about anything, from politics to religion to the very best toppings for pizza. (Pineapple pizza, for the record, is an abomination in the eyes of the Lord.)

But the one thing we can pretty much all agree on is that 99.99% of what we do in the bathroom, we want to do in absolute privacy. No matter what it is that's brought you in there—whether it's related to health, hygiene, grooming, or digestion—chances are you'd recoil like a vampire in sunlight if somebody were to suddenly fling the bathroom door wide open and catch you mid...whatever.

And yet, humans are social animals, and we almost never completely lose our desire for companionship, even when we're engaged in the most private of private acts. That's why so many of us keep our bathrooms stocked with books or transistor radios, or even bring smartphones in, so that even during these most isolated of moments, we can nevertheless remain connected with the outside world.

Not that any of these are a true or adequate substitute for the living, breathing real thing.

Enter the not-so-humble housecat.

I hear from cat-moms and cat-dads all the time who are thoroughly mystified as to *why*, exactly, little Coco or Smokey will insist on following them into the bathroom, and *I'm* always thoroughly mystified by their mystification. Because the truth is that your cat doesn't give a flying fig *what* you're doing in there, so long as she gets to be with you—her very favorite being in the entire universe—while you do it.

It's easy (and painful) to imagine a scenario wherein somebody walks into the bathroom, catches you in the middle of some less-than-attractive act and, as a result, never looks at you quite the same way again.

But there isn't a single thing you could do in the bathroom, or in any room, that would be so odd, off-putting, or downright repulsive that it would make your cat love you one iota less, or judge you to be one less particle awesome than she already thinks you are. She just wants to hang, is all. She's happier being with you than without you, no matter how many raw veggies may currently be working their way through your system. And, that being the case, she simply doesn't understand why you feel the occasional need to disrupt your closer-than-closeness with a resolutely shut bathroom door.

Nobody, in other words, will ever make you feel more known—or less judged—than your cat will. Your cat really and truly *sees* you, all the way down to your literal bottom, and loves you just the same, regardless. She understands that while love may not always be pretty, loving someone only at their most attractive isn't really love at all.

So break out the nose-hair trimmer, uncap the Preparation H, unspool the toilet paper (if your cat hasn't already thoughtfully provided this service), and leave the bathroom door open for kitty to join you if she feels like it. And know, as you do so, that you're the insanely fortunate object of a love that's bona fide, limitless, and one-hundred-percent unconditional in the truest sense of the word.

And that's as **PAWSOME** as it gets!

You're the only one who truly understands your cat

C ats have a reputation for weirdness that's probably not *entirely* deserved. Still, even the most die-hard cat lover would have to admit that cats, at times, can be just the teensiest bit odd.

While many of those little oddities become more explicable the more you understand cats generally, each individual cat has his or her own little *purr*sonality quirks that nobody could ever hope to understand—nobody, that is, other than *you*, the person who knows your cat best.

Only you will know that Mr. Whiskers is unhappy unless permitted to paw open the bottom bathroom sink cabinet and then curl inside it for a nap, or that you're not allowed to refill an ice-cube tray without taking a few of the frozen cubes out for Binx to play "hockey" with, or that Cali waits to walk *down* the stairs until you start walking *up* the stairs so she can pass you at the precise halfway point, or that Tucker insists on licking dry-cleaner's bags, or that Fiona will curl up on a pile of potholders on your kitchen counter to take a nap, but will emphatically *not* be happy if those potholders are replaced with dish towels...

And so on. You get the point.

Over the years, I've stopped asking *why???* when it comes to these small idiosyncrasies that comprise my cats' personalities—rather, I cherish my status as the sole person who can understand them all, and who can make them explicable to other people. (*Clayton won't take one of those treats unless you place it in the precise center of an empty dish*, I always have to remind my husband.)

It's just one more hallmark of the uniquely close and **PAWSOME** relationship that you—and you alone—have with your cat.

Cats will never mock your taste in music

C onfession: My guilty-pleasure playlist is embarrassing twice over—both for the specific songs on it, and also for just how much information about my age (ahem) it reveals. Its highlights (or lowlights) include "I Can't Hold Back" by Survivor, "Fight Fire With Fire" by Kansas, "Good Vibrations" by Marky Mark and the Funky Bunch, "Wannabe" by the Spice Girls, and various tracks by Milli Vanilli. (Yes! I liked Milli Vanilli in college! Sue me!)

There's almost nobody around whom I'd feel comfortable blasting "Strut" by Sheena Easton while dancing around my living room—nobody, that is, except my cats, who don't judge me at all for what I listen to in the privacy of my own home, and who never ever ever try to lecture me on the superior merits of Brian Eno or King Crimson. So long as the *Xanadu* soundtrack isn't blaring loud enough to wake the neighbors, my cats are entirely copacetic.

(They also never do that "howl-along" thing that dogs sometimes do—like my childhood dog Brandi did to Richard Marx songs—which always strikes me as kind of judgey.)

Fun fact: "MMMBop" by Hanson was all over the radio the summer I adopted my blind cat Homer, and it still brings back **PAWSOME** memories whenever I hear it!

Cats love how you look, even on bad hair days

S ome people live hand to mouth. I, apparently, live haircut to haircut. I never fully appreciated just how thin a line separated me from disaster until the state of New Jersey went into lockdown in March 2020 and took my March 21st salon appointment with it.

I have a lot of hair. A *lot* of hair. Hair that's very thick, and very curly, and that grows as rapidly as if my head were a Play-Doh Fuzzy Pumper.

For the first three weeks following my (desperately needed!) missed haircut, things weren't so bad. I was in a kind of '80s-hair-band zone of almost-passable—especially if you were into the whole nostalgia thing. By ten weeks, my bangs had grown so long over my eyes that I could no longer see well enough to drive a car. (Not that it really mattered, since there was no nothing to drive to, anyway.)

By the time quarantine hit the six-month mark, I was Cousin Itt.

Eventually I got vaccinated and could rejoin the outside world, at which point even my entirely non-judgmental husband was looking forward to my first post-lockdown haircut. But I can think of two fuzzy little somebodies to whom the chaotic state of my hair for so many months never made one lick of difference.

That's because cats—much more than even the most adoring person in your life—really and truly don't care *at all* what you look like. How you look never had a single thing to do with how your cat felt about you in the first place, or the very, *very* positive impression they formed of you way back in the beginning of your relationship. So there's absolutely no reason for their opinions to be shaped *now* by something as entirely inconsequential as the ever-changing state of your hair—not even on a hair day so *very* bad that looking in the mirror makes you want to crawl right back into bed.

Not that your cat will ever think getting back into bed is a bad idea.

PAWSOME!

Loving a cat means always having to say you're sorry

I've never bought the oft-vaunted idea that love means never having to say you're sorry. On the contrary, I've always believed that true love means knowing when you owe the one you love an apology, and then offering that apology sincerely and without hesitation.

Nevertheless, it can be hard to swallow your pride and humbly admit you were wrong. If you're fortunate enough to live with a cat, however, you'll have lots of opportunities to practice—because cats always know *exactly* what you've done wrong.

Here's a handy list of things I've done to irritate my own cats over the years—and that you, more likely than not, have done to irritate yours—to give you a head start. Simply fill in the blank with the appropriate answer or answers. You'll be apologizing like a pro in no time!

"I'm sorry, Muffin, for [blank]"

Waking you up
Breathing too loudly
Sneezing too loudly
Taking your spot on the couch
Sleeping on your side of the bed
Shifting positions while you were napping on top of me
Closing the bathroom door while you were still outside

Closing the bathroom door while you were still inside

Closing any door, at any time, for any reason

Paying attention to the computer/smartphone/television screen instead of you

Touching your toes

Kissing your nose

Rubbing your belly

Petting you with wet hands

Cuddling with Patches longer than I cuddled with you

Singing the Mentos jingle without realizing I was doing it

Meowing back at you

Feeding you too early, too late, and/or with an unacceptable new brand of food

Picking you up

Putting you down

Looking at you funny

Letting the neighbor cat look at you funny

Letting the birds outside look at you funny

Allowing noisy children to ride their bicycles on the sidewalk in front of our house

Anything else not on this list that I may have forgotten

All of the above

Cats: Patiently helping us iron out our kinks, flaws, and very human failings for going on ten millennia now.
PAWSOME!

Cats wash their privates in public because they straight-up don't give AF

T he typical American is never going to be as comfortable on a topless beach as the average French person. And as for being okay with public nudity (or a level of clothes-less-ness that's practically nudity), Brazilians, particularly during *carnivale,* have us all beat.

But when it comes to fully splaying and displaying all the hidden nooks and crannies of one's own body, absolutely nobody can hold even the tiniest candle to your cat. Your cat who will wait until you have ten people over for a dinner party, climb right into the middle of the dining-room table where every single one of your guests can't help but watch her, casually hoist one hind leg high in the air—offering the kind of "panoramic" view of all the goodies that, among humans, is usually reserved for the doctor's office or waxing salon—and *go to town* for long, *long* minutes with the scouring power of her own pink tongue.

No shame. No inhibitions. Absolutely no rats' asses given.

Like a *boss.*

Because that's what **PAWSOME** looks like.

Cats force you to keep doors open

I once saw a cartoon of a cat standing before the pearly gates of Heaven, with an obviously irritated St. Peter holding them open and admonishing the cat, "Make up your mind! Are you going in or not?"

Below was a caption that read: *How cats end up with nine lives.*

Cats never seem able to make up their minds if they want to be inside or outside. Even indoor-only cats like mine will cry and cry at a closed bedroom door and then, once you've opened the door to let them pass and closed it again behind them, will immediately begin caterwauling anew—only this time from the other side.

But I think that looking at it from such a binary, A/B perspective sort of misses the point. Your cat wants to be both in *and* out—which may sound contradictory, but really just means your cat wants their options to be as open as that door you're so determined to close.

While we do all inevitably have to make choices in life, closing ourselves off from options too quickly—along with new people, new ideas, and new ways of looking at the world—often means we end up jumping at the first thing that comes along, which is a sucker bet your cat would *never* take.

Or, to put it another way, life is often better with open doors.

Also, I suspect that cats secretly find it amusing to watch us jump up and down every thirty seconds, growing more and more exasperated, while they try to make up their minds on the whole in/out question.

It just goes to prove what we've always secretly suspected: Cats have a sense of humor.

PAWSOME!

Cats' purrs prevent heart attacks and help heal bones, muscles, and tendons

S ome people say that laughter is the best medicine. My mom is apt to scoff and insist that, in fact, *medicine* is the best...well, you know. But my mom has a certain tendency toward literal-mindedness, which doesn't stop her from being lots of fun at parties.

Whichever side of the question you come down on, cats have got you covered. Not only do they keep us in figurative stitches as talented natural comedians, but they also help keep us *out* of *literal* stitches, because cats' purrs have the actual, honest-to-gosh ability to make us healthier and help us heal from injuries faster.

There's even science to prove it.

Cats' purrs tend to vibrate at a frequency of between 20 to 150 Hertz (Hz), a range that's been associated with all sorts of health benefits. Vibrations in that range, according to *Scientific American,* can facilitate bone density and the healing of injured bones, muscles, and tendons. According to a 2018 article in *Orthopedics This Week,* research on frequencies that promote bone growth, fracture healing, pain relief, and relief of inflammation show that frequencies between 20 Hz and 150 Hz are healing frequencies. Vibrations in this range can also help decrease the effects of dyspnea (difficulty breathing) in both humans and other cats.

Not convinced yet that cats have magical healing powers? Then consider this: A 2016 study by the University of Minnesota found that cat owners are 40% less likely to suffer heart attacks or cardiovascular disease as compared to owners of other types of pets or non pet owners, and a Canadian study from 2015 published in *Psychology Today* states that living with a cat can lower cholesterol as effectively as medication. A three-year study at the Baker Medical Research Institute in Melbourne, Australia has shown that living with a cat can lower triglycerides, and a State University of New York at Buffalo study found that cat lovers are likelier to have lower blood pressure, reduced heart rate, and less anxiety as opposed to those poor, spiritually impoverished souls living a cat-free existence.

It goes without saying that you should always consult your own doctor before pursuing any course of, or alternative to, medical treatment. Nevertheless, the fact remains that cat lovers don't just live *better* (of course we do—we live with cats!), we also live *longer*.

Who could ask for anything more?

PAWSOME!

Cats' teeny-tiny noses are the height of aesthetic perfection

Especially when they're freckly...

Sometimes they're even shaped like little hearts!

PAWSOME!

Cats love to get high

N ormally, "loves to get high" wouldn't exactly be an attractive quality in a living companion. And far be it for me to advocate—or even appear to advocate—for the recreational use of narcotics. Cats may be people too, but people most definitely aren't cats—and what's harmless and endearing in a cat can be anywhere from completely annoying (I say this as the unfortunate alumnus of several college-era relationships with stoner boyfriends) to downright deadly if replicated in humans.

Having gotten that caveat out of the way, however, I'm asking that you please not harsh my mellow—because there's very little in this life as utterly and insanely adorable as the sight of one's normally graceful, self-possessed kitty rolling and flipping with wild-eyed abandon while under the influence of that wacky feline weed *nepeta cataria*, otherwise known as catnip.

If getting my cats get high on catnip is wrong, then I don't wanna be right.

Catnip is a perennial herb that's a member of the mint family—albeit one that produces very different effects from what one normally sees with mint. (No matter how much mint chocolate chip ice cream I consume, it rarely makes me fall to the ground and roll around in pure, unrestrained delight.) The chemical compound that attracts and affects cats is called nepetalactone—which is found in the leaves and stems—although it should be noted that not all cats are responsive to 'nip, and almost no cats younger than six months old are.

But, having lived with five cats who *lost their flipping minds* whenever a pile of catnip or a catnip toy was put in front of them (they were particularly turned on by Maui Meow loose catnip and the *Yeowww!* line of catnip toys), I can tell you that watching a cat get silly on the 'nip is one of the great, great joys of kitty custodianship.

Nepetalactone is a stimulant when sniffed by cats, producing a "high" that's been described in studies as similar to either marijuana or LSD (which scientists figured out...how, exactly?). It's perfectly safe for cats, although eating an excessive amount can lead to stomach upset. And catnip may even have some beneficial effects for humans. When brewed into a tea it has a mildly calming effect similar to chamomile; it's also known to make an effective and nontoxic mosquito repellant.

Not that any of this would justify bogarting your cat's stash. A tea that smooths out your jangled nerves is all well and good, but the entertainment value of watching your beloved kitty companion tumble across the floor in pure catnip abandon?

That's **PAWSOME**!

Head bonks

Like many of you, I have one cat (this would be Clayton, my "tripod") who's our home's self-appointed official greeter. He's the one waiting smack in the middle of the doorway when my husband and I walk in, who immediately introduces himself to any and all newcomers, who gallops over to give returning visitors an enthusiastic "howdedoo!" and warm their laps the moment they've sat down.

Clayton is also our household's dispenser of head bonks—more properly referred to as "head bunting"—which makes a lot of sense, because head bonking is deeply social behavior. So much of what our kitties do to demonstrate their fondness for us seems to come down to the communal sharing of scents, and the same is true with head bonks. When your cat butts you with his head, he's basically attempting to transfer scent from his own forehead scent glands (located in those sparse patches of fur between eye and ear) onto you—not so much to "mark" you, per se, as to make sure the two of you smell alike. You *are* a family, after all.

In the wild, it's the most confident and social cat in the community who goes around head-bonking all the other cats, to make sure everyone has the same scent. Which is why it makes so much sense that Clayton greets and bonks all newcomers within minutes of entry—Clayton's apparent mission in life being to singlehandedly dispel all those rumors about feline "aloofness" and corral as many people as he can into his ever-expanding feline/human herd.

But even without all the scientific explain-y stuff, you already knew intuitively that, when your cat bonks you with his head, that's his way of saying, "I love you."

PAWSOME

Out of all the humans in the world, your cat chose you

While cats will sometimes condescend to live under less-than-ideal circumstances (*somebody* with opposable thumbs has to open those tuna cans, after all), cats—unlike dogs—feel no particular need to bestow their affections on any unworthy object.

Moreover, cats are keen observers of human nature—they can "read" our body language, the tone of our voice, and even our smell and the dilation of our pupils for information about what kind of mood we're in and the thoughts that are running through our brain.

So a cat that loves you (and you'll certainly be able to tell if one does!) doesn't love you because she *needs* to, but because she *chooses* to.

And, given how *purr*ceptive your finicky feline is, if she's chosen *you* out of all the humans on earth as a worthy object for her affections, chances are that you are a pretty exceptional human!

PAWSOME!

Cats are amazing at receiving affection

This one might almost feel like I'm damning cats with faint praise. After all 'tis easier to receive than to give, right?

Most of us, though, actually find it much *harder* to take than to give. We tend to be afraid of seeming like we need too much. Which is silly, since we don't love our cats *less* because of how much attention and affection they're willing to accept from us. We love them more for it! Nobody, upon feeling a blissed-out cat lean harder into their hand and purr in delight, thinks, *This is certainly a bummer.*

Cats remind us that it's okay to accept kind gestures without immediately worrying about how to reciprocate—or to demand immediate reciprocation for our own kind gestures. No one sits there with a ledger book, after all, and counts up all the times they've petted or fed their cat versus the number of great things our cats have done for *us.*

Our cats do the greatest thing of all just by letting us love them. And they know intuitively that, when it comes to the ones we love who truly love us in return, it all comes out even in the end.

In the meantime, it's totally acceptable—and even kinda **PAW-SOME**—to ask the ones we love for a little extra care when we need it.

Cats keep cat haters out of your life

I think there's something genuinely wrong with people who hate cats.

Naturally I realize there are people who, simply as a matter of taste, don't really care for cats. That's not what I'm talking about. I mean the people who flat-out *loathe* cats and take some sort of weird pride in talking *ad nauseam* about their particular affliction. Like the guy who cornered me at a cocktail party once, six months before my memoir about my blind cat was published, and spent a full ten minutes going on and on and *on* about how much he and his wife hated cats.

Look, I may not *love* goats. I don't especially want to hang out with goats. But I understand why goats *exist* and why some people have them. I don't feel like I have to launch into a whole "Goats Are The Worst" diatribe any time somebody offers me a goat cheese salad, just because one time, when I was six, a goat once tried to eat all the hair off my head during a petting-zoo field trip.

Cat haters have a screw loose, is what I'm saying. Scratch the surface of the typical cat hater and you're almost certain to find any number of other deal-breaking character deficiencies: stinginess, pettiness, bad manners, and lord knows what else.

Unfortunately, much like serial killers, cat haters tend to look and talk and act just like you and me. You may not even realize you're deep into conversation with such a profoundly maladjusted person, or working side by side with one, or even (heaven forfend!) about to accept a second date with one, until it's way too late.

This is where your cat has got you covered. If the mere mention of Puss in conversation causes someone's nose to wrinkle with distaste, then you know what you're dealing with. If such a person somehow manages to make it across the threshold of your home unsuspected, the expression of alarm and aversion upon seeing your cat tree will tell you all you need to know about not issuing a *second* invitation.

Not that they'd be likely to accept that invitation, anyway. When it comes to keeping cat haters and other reprobates well beyond your property line, there will never be a better home-security system than your cat.

Heck, a true and unrepentant cat hater might even start avoiding you in *public* places—just to make one hundred percent sure they never again run the risk of running into, or hearing about, your cat. Which is probably the ideal outcome, anyway. I mean, what use do you even have for a joyless, soulless, mental defective like that?

Your cat has just done you the biggest favor ever by giving them the old Puss-in-boot straight out the front door and out of your life, never to be seen or heard from again.

Pretty **PAWSOME**, no?

Cats love drama

It often surprises me that there aren't more feline stars of the stage and screen, because probably nobody you know has more of an innate sense of drama than your cat.

In fairness, though, I'd hate to be the director trying to give a cat acting notes. (*Ginger, darling, I'm wondering if you could give me juuuuust a hint of disdain...narrow your eyes in disgust for me...a little more...just a bit more...yes! Just the way you're looking at me right now! That's PERFECT!*)

And yet it hardly seems to matter that fewer cats see their names in lights than ought to—because when you're a cat, all the world's a stage anyway.

Shut a cat out of the bedroom or bathroom and she'll either howl at the door in anguish (*WHYYYYYYYYYYYYYYY?!!?!?*) or else mew so sadly and plaintively that it sounds as if her very soul is being ripped from her body. Try rubbing your kitty's tempting tummy when she's not in the mood for belly rubs, and she won't just bat your hand away—she'll wrap her entire body around it (teeth included!) as if she were fighting off a life-threatening attack. And if you've ever seen a cat locked in a life-and-death battle with an inanimate toy mouse—flinging it about the room so he can "chase" it down—then you know exactly what I'm talking about.

A cat about to accidentally tumble off a couch will dig her claws in and cling to the cushion as if it were the precipice of a yawning abyss threatening to swallow her up forever. Put food down in front of a cat that he doesn't like, and he'll either take one sniff and recoil forcefully—as if you'd just placed a dish of rotten eggs in front of him—or else begin making frantic digging/burying motions around it, as if to say, *Cover this up! IT'S HIDEOUS!!!*

The *truly* dramatic cat will do both.

There's no doubt about it—the typical cat is the star of her very own reality show that exists only in her head. It can sometimes be exhausting just trying to keep up.

On the other hand, what would we ever do without all the **PAW-SOME** entertainment?

Cats have inspired great artists for centuries

E gyptians were painting cats on the walls of temples and tombs five thousand years ago, and Chinese artists were painting cats well before that.

It's not hard to understand why those with a heightened aesthetic sensibility would find in*purr*ation in *felis catus*—effortlessly elegant, compact and graceful (usually), cats are the visual equivalent of poetry.

Here, then, is a brief and by no means complete sampling of some of world's most famous artists who've also been unashamed ailurophiles:

Leonardo da Vinci, Henri Matisse, Frida Kahlo, Pablo Picasso, Salvador Dali, Andy Warhol, Ai Weiwei, Maya Lin, Jean-Michel Basquiat, Gustav Klimt, Paul Klee, Edward Gorey, Pierre Bonnard, Marcel Duchamp, Balthus, Hedda Sterne, Frank Stella, Jay DeFeo, Beatrice Wood, Emily Barto, and Georgia O'Keefe.

Great minds think alike—and some of the greatest artistic minds ever were convinced that cats are utterly, thoroughly, inspirationally **PAWSOME!**

Cats have the fluffiest, mushiest bellies ever

However fluffy your cat may be on her back and along her sides, her belly is guaranteed to be *twice* as fluffy—and fuzzy, and just so incredibly yummy and soft.

Which makes it soooooooooooooooo vexing that most cats will spring at your hand like a bear trap if you so much as *try* to rub those tempting tummies!

Still, that moment when your cat rolls over on her back and exposes her belly in all its fleecy, feathery, furry glory?

Totally **PAWSOME!**

Sometimes cats sit like couch potatoes

Who can blame them for trying to get comfy when they work so hard all day being **PAWSOME** for us???

Cats will help you make the bed

There are people who find actual joy, and a certain amount of Zen calm, in doing housework. I freely admit that I am not one of them. Watching one of those "let's clean the house!" montages in some family movie—the kind where everybody from mom and dad down to the littlest rug-rat grabs a broom or bucket and cheerfully pitches in, while the power-guitar chords of _This Is Family Fun!_ strum insistently in the background—I'll turn to my husband and say, "So...I guess this is a movie about a bunch of people who all got lobotomized at the same time?"

But there's one household chore that I actually look forward to every week, and that's when it comes time to change the sheets.

Nobody has ever told my cats that housework is kind of a bummer, or that changing sheets even qualifies as housework, so they experience every part of the process with undiluted joy. As soon as I pull the new sheets from the linen closet, they know what's up—racing ahead of me into the bedroom where they stare at the bed with pupils dilated to murderous proportions. _We're going to kill those sheets so hard!_ I yank off the blankets and begin to pull at the old sheets as my cats leap right into the middle of the mattress and cling ferociously, holding on with all their claws as I drag both sheets and cats off the bed. _Wheeeeeeeee!_ I can almost hear them thinking as they soar briefly into the air—two little genies on a magic carpet ride—before landing on the ground. _This is FUN!_

The fun doesn't stop there! How would I even be able to ensure that the new, clean sheets I put onto the bed were straight and airtight without my helpful kitties racing from one corner of the mattress to the other to double-check my work? Sure, it takes twice as long as necessary to accomplish this task—what with my cats burrowing under the fitted sheet as I attempt to smooth it out, or forming their bodies into tight lumps beneath the top sheet and blanket, or bunching up the blanket into a big enough clump that they can lie on their sides and kick at it with their back legs "bunny feet" style, until finally I cry, "Come *on*, you guys!"

If cats could high-five, my cats would definitely be high-fiving on their way out of the bedroom. *We showed those sheets who's boss!*

It's the most mundane of mundane tasks, but the wide-eyed delight with which my cats greet this weekly chore lends an undeniably festive air to the proceedings.

As if it were an unexpected day off from school, or a trip to an amusement park.

PAWSOME!

Cats have selflessly provided us with millions of hours of free online entertainment

There are literally millions of cats on the internet. They caper endearingly for our amusement on YouTube, Tik Tok, Instagram, and Facebook. They're featured players in memes, gifs, and online greeting cards. There are tens of thousands of websites devoted to cat pictures, cat health, cat products, et cetera.

And yet, there aren't actually any cats *on* the Internet, if you see what I mean. They don't log in themselves to any of the many social media accounts opened in their names. They don't browse the web or swipe through apps or chuckle at the umpteenth photo of a cat wearing a silly costume or whose face is, inexplicably, surrounded by a piece of bread. (Why was that a thing, again?)

Which means that everything cats do to entertain us online, they do solely for our benefit. All the many, many hours cats devote to posing, scampering, donning funny hats, falling off of tables, hiding under blankets, knocking things off of counters, meowing in tune to "Twinkle, Twinkle, Little Star," swimming in the ocean, riding skateboards, fighting with dogs over sofa cushions, trying to squeeze into too-small cardboard boxes, walking on their hind legs, soothing fussy babies to sleep, playing the piano—*et cetera*—they do purely out of the goodness of their hearts. Just to make us happy.

Who else gives so much and asks so little in return?

Nobody, that's who.

One more reason why cats are as **PAWSOME** as it gets!

Cats don't make you feel bad when you leave, but they're psyched when you get home

Back when I was a teenaged babysitter, I remember having temporary charge of many a tiny tot who would wail and sob disconsolately when their parents headed out for the evening. And my own childhood dog Casey—who was particularly attached to me, and who remains the single greatest dog I've ever lived with—would, according to my mom, howl at the front door to our house for a good twenty minutes whenever I disappeared through it.

Not every child or dog reacts quite so dramatically, of course, to routine leave-takings. Still, it's enough to make you appreciate the relative casualness with which our cats greet our departures to work or the store or out for drinks with friends. "See you later, Mittens!" you might call over your shoulder on your way out, only to be rewarded for this small courtesy with a) a blank stare; b) the slight flickering of one eyelid from a cat who's far too deep into a catnap to care even a little about *your* comings and goings; or c) literally nothing at all, because your cat isn't even anywhere in the vicinity of the door to see you off. Why should he be? It's not as if your departure will adversely affect his sleeping schedule—which, if we're being honest, is most housecats' top-of-mind concern at least eighty percent of the time.

And yet, the sleepy-eyed indifference with which your cats see you off couldn't be further from the glad giddiness they greet you with upon your return—the joyful bounding to the door, the leaping and cavorting when you walk through it. They'll race down the stairs or up from the basement or out from under the bed just so they can be correctly positioned to greet you with a lusty *MEOW!* and an ecstasy of head-bonks against your leg the very moment you cross the threshold.

Perhaps it's true that absence makes the heart grow fonder. Maybe while you were gone, your cat had time to wonder, *What if she* never *comes back? WHO WILL FEED ME???* Or perhaps, even though it's a ritual that's repeated day in and day out, the fact that you've returned strikes your cat as being miraculous all anew—just like we humans have those moments when, as we look at the sleeping cat curled up in our lap, it seems far too good to be true that Fate saw fit to bring us together.

In any case, living with a cat means nobody will ever try to lay a guilt trip on you when you head out into the great world beyond your front door. But a furry little someone will always be very, *very* happy to greet you when you return, worn and weary, to the warmth of your own home.

PAWSOME!

The cute and careful way cats lap ice cream from a spoon

I f you've ever given your dog table scraps, then you know it is, to a certain extent, a risky endeavor.

For one thing, dogs can be inept at distinguishing fingers from the food dangling at the ends of those fingers—meaning you have to exercise a fair amount of caution, even when indulging a relatively small dog.

Don't get me wrong—I'm a dog lover from way back. Nevertheless, it provides a striking counterpoint for the very thoughtful, very deliberate manner in which your cat approaches something like ice cream being offered on a spoon.

After a judicious period of preliminary sniffing and head tilting (trying, no doubt, to determine the best angle of approach), his little pink tongue will dab at the ice cream very delicately and carefully, with much apparent seriousness devoted to the whole endeavor. My own cats look downright professorial when offered ice cream on a spoon, as if somewhere in their minds they're covering a blackboard with a complex series of equations—*Good Will Hunting* style—while they mentally hammer out the optimal methodology for transferring the frosty treat from spoon to belly. *Perhaps if I turn my head <u>perpendicular</u> to the spoon...*

This thoughtful circumspection, however, will in no way guarantee that a tiny dot of ice cream doesn't end up on your kitty's nose.

And that, my feline-loving friend, is the most **PAWSOME** part!

Cats are natural comedians

C ats are hilarious. It's a fact so indisputable that even people who don't care for cats (but who are nevertheless aware that the internet exists, and that 50% of it is comprised of funny cat videos) would have a hard time denying it—which should make the writing of this particular entry a breeze.

But it's nowhere near as easy as it should be. Partly that's because nothing saps the funny right out of something like trying to explain *why* it's funny. Complicating things further is that there are so many different, and frequently contradictory, theories about cats' innate humorousness. Some say cats are funny because they act so pompous and dignified, while others say it's because cats are so goofy. Some say it's because cats are cute and others say it's because cats *aren't* cute (cats are very serious creatures, doncha know).

Perhaps it's the mystery itself that makes them so amusing.

The one hypothesis that seems closest to the mark is that cats are always *getting into* something. Getting into things on a regular basis, all by itself, will create tons of opportunities for wackiness and hilarity. After all, there aren't any sitcoms whose weekly plots revolve around characters sitting quietly on their living room couch, doing exactly what they're supposed to be doing. Getting into trouble is every cat's specialty and birthright.

So when cats accidentally close themselves into cardboard boxes, root around—tush up—in your bottom dresser drawer, climb to the top of the refrigerator to take a nap and promptly roll right off it, walk on tiptoe around the toilet bowl until they accidentally fall in, or redistribute freshly cleaned socks from the laundry basket to various hidden corners throughout the house, they're simply fulfilling their manifest destiny.

Ultimately, though, maybe it's best to adopt a philosophy of *why ask why?* Cats are hilarious because they *are*. And they've consented to live among us humans—bumbling and foolish though we may be—to keep us laughing through good times and bad.

PAWSOME!

Cats make being lazy look soooooo good...

D oing stuff is overrated.

I realize that's an unpopular point of view in these over-caffeinated, over-stimulated, over-scheduled times. Nevertheless, I remain firm in my opinion that sunny days do *not* have to be spent outdoors, early birds do *not* get all the worms worth having, and devoting entire hours to letting your mind wander will not only add years onto your life—it's also just an inherently good and worthwhile thing to do.

Nobody knows the value of doing nothing at all better than your cat. I talk a lot in this book about the sheer volume of hours cats will spend napping. But if you look at the hours that your cat spends fully awake, it's not like they're especially "productive" or jam-packed with activity. He'll spend at least half of that awake time watching the world outside your windows, or observing you while you perform some cheerless human task like answering emails or mopping the kitchen—or else he's staring off into the middle distance at nothing in particular, thinking about nobody knows what.

The reason why your cat can get away with a level of loafing that, let's face it, you and I could never pull off without being called lazy is because your cat does it with so much *style* as to be above reproach. Cats are natural aristocrats, with their physical grace and ever-so-slightly-aloof 'tudes. Their effortless elegance can't help but make you a bit reticent to call them out for being lazy, or question why they're doing—or *not* doing—something at any given moment. (*Who are you to question me?!*)

And even the cats like my Clayton, who are, perhaps, more aptly described as "doofy" than "deep," are still so very endearing that what else would you even *want* them to do other than sit there being their lovable selves?

The point is that if you want to work a certain amount of laziness into your day-to-day lifestyle (and I really think you should), you'll never find a better Zen-master to not only show you how to do it, but how to *get away with it*, than your very own cat.

Study laziness diligently enough at the paws of your feline guru, and people won't think you're a shiftless loafer when you lounge about—catlike and elegant—doing nothing in particular.

They'll just think you're **PAWSOME!**

Cats make excellent negotiating partners

Negotiations can often be a tense and drawn-out affair. The Hawaiian people have a solution for extreme stalemates called *ho'oponopono*. Basically, the parties to the dispute go into a room and aren't allowed to come back *out* of that room until an agreement has been reached.

Fortunately, nothing that dramatic is required where your cat is concerned. You may have heard just the opposite. Perhaps somebody once told you that cats are stubborn, unreasonable creatures. That an aggrieved cat might slash your sofa, poop in your shoes, or keep you up with her yowling all night just to punish you for not letting her get her own way.

Allow me to assure you that nothing could be further from the truth.

Whether you're haggling over a change in feeding schedule (*Pretty please, Socks, no more 5:00 am breakfasts...*), trying to wangle more time in the comfiest living room easy chair (*C'mon, Snowball—can't I just sit here during NCIS?*), or attempting to retain the entirety of your freshly made tuna sandwich, *any* cat can be negotiated with—quickly and decisively—by following this simple, two-step procedure:

Step 1: Give your cat whatever she wants.

Step 2: End negotiation.

See? Easy, peasy, **PAWSOME!**

Cats' toes look like beans

They're toes! But, somehow, also beans!

PAWSOME!

Cats never abandon you during the tough times

Whoever said, *Laugh and the world laughs with you, cry and you cry alone,* clearly never lived with a cat.

Inevitably in life there will be dark days—days when it feels as if even the people you love most have betrayed you or disappeared altogether. Days when all the news is bad and nobody will return your calls. Days when it feels as if there isn't a single friendly face anywhere to be found.

But if you live with a cat, you never have to look far.

Dogs have a well-deserved reputation for loyalty, which nobody in their right mind would try to dispute. But I always find the loyalty of cats to be more remarkable. Dogs are more naturally "hardwired" for group ties, for starters, whereas cats are solitary hunters who spook easily and dislike having their habits altered. And yet they've consented to live in our company, to put up with the sounds of televisions and garbage disposals and cars racing by outside. They stick by us when we move homes, get married, have babies, bring home more cats or even (gasp!) puppies to invade their territory.

And let's face it—for all the guff we give cats for being "mysterious" and "difficult" creatures to live with—it's not as if, from a cat's perspective, we're so easy to predict or figure out ourselves.

We don't necessarily make it easy for them, is what I'm saying.

Nevertheless, they stick by us. They might get anxious at times—and they'll certainly let us know when they do!—but they continue to purr right alongside us whether our paychecks rise or fall, our families grow or shrink, our surroundings become fancier or shabbier with the passage of years. Even on days when you hear a disheartening round of, "I'd *love* to be there for you if only I could..." your cat will be a rock-solid presence by your side.

No matter what.

Nowhere else will you find so much unconditional love and loyalty wrapped up in such a fuzzy, adorable, purring little package.

A cat's unwavering loyalty is about as **PAWSOME** as it gets.

Cats bring a touch of the wild into our lives

A re cats domesticated? is one of the most frequently Googled questions about cats—at least, judging by Google's autocomplete suggestions. Which implies that, as much as we typically think of cats as being "domestic" animals, deep down we're not *entirely* sure they are.

That ambivalence probably reflects a certain amount of truth. A growing body of evidence suggests that humans didn't so much domesticate cats as cats began to domesticate themselves—availing themselves of the abundant rodents we attracted when we invented farming—around 10,000 years ago (which sounds like a long time, but is still only a fraction of the time that dogs, for example, have been domesticated). And cats didn't even start morphing into household companions who lived indoors with us—as opposed to in our barns or around our grain silos—until about two hundred years ago, which is when humans first began consciously breeding cats for certain traits. In contrast, we've been breeding dogs to be less wolf-like for 30,000 years or even longer, by some estimates.

This is all by way of saying that the sense you sometimes get—as you see your little "house panther" slinking about the living room, looking for all the world like an actual panther or bobcat shrunk down to lap-sized cuteness—that your cat is equal parts wild animal and house pet is probably accurate. Since cats have, quite literally, done more to train us to do *their* bidding than vice versa, there's only so much of their innate wildness that they've had, or wanted, to give up.

I recently asked my readers on Facebook what their favorite thing about living with a cat was. The answers ranged from *You expect me to pick just one?!!?* to *My cat loves me unconditionally.* And then there was one person who wrote this:

Having a murder-mitten equipped ninja running through the house who then suddenly decides he needs to snuggle in my lap.

So the next time you feel your life is too tame, too constrained, too stultifyingly predictable, make a mental note to spend more time with your cat.

She remembers where the wild things are—and, if you're lucky, she'll let you know, too.

PAWSOME!

Cats chase their own tails

C'mon, you've seen it. It's like your very own clown show on the living room floor. And the angrier they seem to be getting at their own tails, the funnier it is to us.

So futile. So goofy. So delightfully **PAWSOME!**

Cats will persuade you not to get too many house plants

It's been my general experience that cats and houseplants don't go super-well together (unless you're growing cat grass—in which case, carry on). Cats are apt to chew on and otherwise maul indoor flora, not to mention the occasional tendency to substitute potting soil for kitty litter. (Yikes!)

It's probably just as well though because, honestly...did you really *want* all those houseplants, anyway?

People will warn you about all the inconveniences involved in adopting any kind of animal companion—the vet bills! the all-weather walks!—but they very rarely warn you about the burdens of keeping plants in your home.

Plants, I've come to learn, are *much* fussier about precise climate control then cats (which is saying something). And it's not like you can just put down a bowl of water and let the plant lap some up whenever it's thirsty—you have to *constantly* be aware of when *this* plant needs to be watered, and when *that* plant needs to be watered, and it's a sure bet that your various plants will have vexingly varied watering needs that you'll have to commit to memory. And when you leave town, forget about it! What friend will be stalwart enough to agree—without any arm-twisting, mind you—to come to your house every day and wade through an entire legal pad's worth of specific instructions regarding each individual plant's daily water intake and sun requirements?

And then there are the studies that say your plants won't grow properly if you don't talk to them all the time. Seriously? Most days I barely even feel like talking to the actual *humans* I know, and now I have to rattle my weary brain at the end of a long workday so I can dredge up appropriate conversational topics for a *houseplant?! Are you kidding me?!!?* Whose genius idea was this?!!?

At least cats are sensible enough to keep growing whether or not you natter nonsense at them all the livelong day..

In conclusion: You're sooooooooooo much better off having cats than lots of houseplants. There's just nothing **PAWSOME** about a home so strewn with vegetation, it looks like an abandoned *Tarzan* set.

Cats help you break in new furniture

There's nothing better, after years of living with the same old junk, than finally treating yourself to a brand-new sofa or recliner. Maybe you spend hours poring over catalogues or driving from store to store on your day off, searching for that one perfect piece that's *so* striking and *so* comfy, you say to yourself, "Here's something I'll be happy to look at and lie on, every day, for the next ten years."

The only problem, once the store's delivery guy has come and gone, is that everything else in your living room suddenly looks so shabby by comparison. Did that divan always list to one side? Was the wood on that coffee table always so dull and scratched up?

Not to worry, though—your cat has you covered! Just give Tabby the Interior-Decorator Cat one week of *fur*ee reign, and soon enough that brand-new addition to your living room will be adorned with a few tasteful claw marks and strategically placed patches of fur.

Not enough to make it look *worn out*, of course. Heavens no! Juuuuuuuust a few thoughtful little touches here and there to make the newcomer blend in seamlessly with the old.

And you won't even have to pay the outrageous rates a professional decorator would demand. Your cat will do the whole job for free—give or take the occasional handful of Greenies.

And that's because your cat is **PAWSOME!**

You can confess absolutely anything to your cat

L oved ones are apt to say, "Nothing you could say would change how I feel about you," but that's probably not strictly true. If, for example, you were to confess to even half your homicidal thoughts following a needlessly and excruciatingly prolonged one-on-one with your boss, you might find yourself squicking others out just a wee bit. Or if your spouse were to call home while away on a business trip to see what you were up to, and you replied, "Oh, you know...sitting around in my underwear eating chocolate chip cookie dough out of the tube," I very much fear that their high opinion of you might, inevitably, be a bit tarnished.

Your cat, on the other hand, has no flying figs to give when it comes to such confessions. I mean, let's face it—eating cookie dough straight out of the tube is still a more productive use of time than about ninety-nine percent of what your cat does all day. And why should homicidal fantasies trouble him when he *actually* killed two rats only a week ago *in real life?* "I did it for fun," your cat would probably tell you, cool as cucumber. "I wasn't even hungry." And while, with very few exceptions, a rat isn't a human being, your cat is probably unwilling to grant that people generally—with the very specific exception of *you*, of course—are all that much more sacred or special than any other type of creature.

The point is, your cat has an unshakeable belief that *you* are among the greatest and most exceptional of human beings ever to walk the earth. What other creature—on four legs or two—could dispense 'nip, treats, or love as well and freely as you do? And, given how exceptionally exceptional you are, what could you possibly confess to your cat that would change his opinion of you one iota?

Not to mention that he probably wouldn't understand most of whatever shameful secret you would admit to him, anyway. My own cats know their names, and the word "lunch," and beyond that it's strictly about facial expressions and tone of voice. "Yes, mommy *did* throw away household garbage in the dumpster behind the grocery store, even though *technically* it's against the law," I might say to them brightly—while administering behind-the-ears scritches, of course—and my cats' sole response would be to purr and gaze at me with the heavy-lidded eyes of feline adoration.

There aren't many relationships in life that will remain one hundred percent rock solid no matter what you confess to. But if you're owned by a cat, then you definitely have at least one.

And that's **PAWSOME!**

Cats meow, mew, coo, chitter, chatter, and whine

L eonardo da Vinci famously said that the smallest feline is a masterpiece.

I'd add that each and every cat is also a symphony—a full-fledged feline orchestra of one, with enough vocal range and differentiation to maintain a running, delightful conversation over the course of a lifetime.

The best part is that no two cats sound exactly alike.

Here, in no particular order, is a partial list of sounds I've observed my cats making over the years, along with an approximate guess-timation as to what each means:

Trill: *Yay! You're about to feed me!*

Chitter: *I would be killing those birds SO HARD if only this stupid window wasn't in the way!*

Coo: *I'm jumping onto the bed/onto the couch/into your lap right now!*

Chatter: *I have something VERY important to tell you. Most likely, it's a report of something you've done wrong—like not feeding me on time. I don't enjoy "scolding" you like this, but it's the only way you'll learn.*

Whine: *You're nooooooooot paying attention to meeeeeeeeeeeeeeeeeeee!*

Mew: *I was sleeping and you woke me; or I want you to pay atten-*

tion to me; or *Gosh, that food you're eating looks yummy!*

Meow: *I'm irritated; I'm hungry; I want attention; You're talking to me, and I'm talking back; You're not talking to me, but I wish you would; Pet me; You're not petting me; You're STILL not petting me! I'm booooooooooored; You're home! I'm so happy to see you! Feed me now; No, seriously, feed me now...*

Pro tip: Be sure to record your cat now; someday you'll be able to play it back and say, "Remember the cute way Muffin used to ask me to pet her? That was **PAWSOME!**"

Cats teach us the importance of holding out for what we really want

Your cat has definite views on everything—not just *some* things, but *every*thing—from the type of food she prefers, to the exact brand of litter she requires, what does (and most certainly does *not*) constitute an acceptable sleeping surface, toys that rock and toys that blow, visitors to your home who are worth her time and those who are *persona non grata*, whether or not you should keep wearing that new perfume you just bought, and also...

It's a list that could go on at some length and encompass all that finds its way before your cat's judgmental eyes.

Suffice it to say that your cat is opinionated. *Very* opinionated.

What's more, she'd rather go hungry, or sleep standing up, or hold her bladder for hours, or be without company for days on end, than bend her exacting standards by even a fraction of an inch.

Don't get me wrong—there's something to be said for not being *too* rigid. A complete unwillingness to compromise is a difficult (not to mention lonely) way to go through life.

By the same token, doesn't it sometimes seem as if we're willing to give up on what we *really* want—and settle for what we secretly believe to be a substandard compromise—a little too easily? Why else would self-help be a billion-dollar industry, based on little more than teaching people how to be more assertive and find the confidence to demand what they truly desire, not just what they'll settle for?

Luckily for you, when it comes to things like being assertive and sticking to your guns, your cat is a certifiable expert—and would be fully willing to enlighten you by example for the entirely reasonable fee of a can of Fancy Feast.

PAWSOME!

Cats help us keep calm and carry on

O ur cats entertain us, they soothe us, and they lull us to sleep with their purrs. They gambol about for our amusement, and they wreak havoc among our framed photos and glass tchotchkes for their own. Yet who could possibly stay mad at them when they look at us with so much love in their eyes?

The reason our cats can look at us with such love and perfect trust, even when things are at their absolute worst, is because they know one great truth—a truth we humans also know, although sometimes we forget that we do:

This too shall pass.

And when it does, things will be **PAWSOME**.

Eventually, we have to say goodbye to them

The late comedian George Carlin once said that every pet is a tiny tragedy waiting to happen. By this, of course, he meant that eventually the day comes—far sooner than we're ready to—when we have to say goodbye.

It's inevitable that all of us cat lovers have moments, over the course of a long life lived with feline companions, when we wish all the way down to our souls that our cats could live as long as we do. While cats actually do live a relatively long time for house pets (and a few years longer than dogs typically do), that fifteen-year average lifespan could double, or even triple, and we wouldn't complain.

I don't want to work too hard to try to spin a negative into a positive. But when I think back on the cats I've been lucky enough to count among my family members, I'm struck by the fact that I was with them when they were teeny-tiny kittens, no more than a few weeks old, and I was also with them in their very last moments of life. And I do find something indescribably beautiful in this cradle-to-grave relationship—something wholly unique, unlike any other we get to have. In no other scenario do we get to see someone through all their firsts in life—perhaps even bottle-feeding them—and also be the one who has the enormous privilege of seeing them off as they breathe their last.

And even for those cats we adopt when they're a bit further along in their life cycle—the opportunity to see them through old age and its aftermath is as filled with warmth, comfort, and love as any sacred responsibility could possibly be.

Almost nothing has ever been harder for me than saying goodbye to the cats I've loved. Nevertheless, my last moments with each of them have been among the most beautiful of my life. I wouldn't trade them—or the memories of them I have today—for anything else in the world.

Perhaps it's the knowledge that our days with our feline companions are always numbered that makes these relationships as magical as they are. There are so many relationships that we take for granted, because deep down we know (or we *think* we know) that we'll have years and years in which to say the things we want to say, or to do the things we want to do together. We'll get in a fight with someone we love and then put off the tendering of apologies, secure in the woefully misguided belief that time is on our side.

The relative brevity of our time with our cats is a drawback, but it's also a gift. It's a reminder that the number of our days here on this earth are, in the end, finite and few.

Which means we have an obligation to make each and every day as **PAWSOME** as we possibly can!

Cats make us better humans

I was walking through an airport gift shop, a few years back, when I caught sight of a greeting card on a display rack that accomplished something no other greeting card I've seen before or since has ever managed to do: It stopped me dead in my tracks. It was a fairly simple card—nothing too fancy or "clever" about it. Beneath a beautiful illustration of a calico cat was the following inscription:

Be The Person Your Cat Thinks You Are.

I bought that greeting card instantly, and to this day I still have it hanging, in a little frame, on the wall above my desk.

We all joke about our cats thinking of us as "servants" or "staff," or regarding us as being incompetent in various ways—particularly when it comes to picking out toys or cat beds that they'll prefer to the bags and boxes said items came in. (*As if a mere human could ever comprehend the twists and turns of the feline mind!*)

But there's a version of me that only my cats see, and I know that it's the best possible version of myself. And while the actual me doesn't always line up with that best-possible me that glows in my cats' eyes, I do find that my cats tend to bring out the best I have to offer.

And while I couldn't say that my relationships with my cats are *better than* my relationships with other people, I will say that experiencing such easy and uncomplicated love—a respite from the more complex, and occasionally bruising, relationships I have with other people—has been a balm on my soul and one of the great joys of my life. And I think (at least, I hope) that I'm a better person for it.

I may never fully succeed in being quite the person my cat think I am. But, thanks to my cat, I do aspire to be a little bit better—and a little more **PAWSOME**—each and every day.

THE HILARIOUS NEXT INSTALLMENT IN THE "PAWSOME" SERIES!

Heartfelt thanks and profound gratitude to the following people (and cats!), without whom I could never have completed this book.

Special thanks to Patti, Nikolaka & Koa!

- » Alyson Amsterdam (and Louie & Biggie)
- » Margaret Auld-Louie (and Julius & Simba)
- » Jamery Sue Barry (and Colby, Sully, Misty & Georgie)
- » Charles Brackney (and Shane, Chloe & Abby)
- » Julie Burns
- » Lisa Calarese (and Riley, Mordecai & Rigby)
- » Deborah Foresman (and Tinkerbell)
- » Paul Froiland (and Louie & Fitzy)
- » Meg Galipault (and Scout, Waffles, Sisu, Dru & Huckleberry)
- » Lee-Ann Gilliam
- » Tracy Ginnane
- » Wanda Goodwin (and Lewie Stewart)
- » Jill Graves
- » Susan Haenicke (and Bessie & Hamilton)
- » Marianne Harding (and Charles Carlos Ambrose Harding)
- » J. Eric Hoehn
- » Susan Anne Kadlec
- » Julie Kennedy
- » Connie Keith-Kerns (and Zoey, Ari Kai & Mrf)

- Calvin & Eileen Keyser (and Ashes, Ninja & Snickers)
- Beth Kirby
- Ken Kistner
- Ronald Koltnow (and Speedy)
- Catherine Larklund
- Louisa Lee
- Carole Loftin (and Sadie, Biscuit & Brazil)
- Julie Lowe (and Gracie, Cougar, Java, Raven, Meeko, & Bella)
- Neta Mercer (and Pouncer, Felix & Snacks)
- TJ Murphy (and Shelly, Max, Gio & Anna)
- David Nagreski (and Chassis)
- Matthew O'Leary (and Hank)
- Melanie Paradise (and Idia)
- Stephanie Peters (and Max)
- D.H. Powell IV (and Bobby & Willow)
- Vanessa Ramirez
- Stephanie Reicen (and Oliver, Mickey & Helen)
- Kathryn Rigsby
- Felicia Roe (and Eurydice & Cassiopeia)
- Janice Rogenski
- Kathy Schlichthernlein (and Scrappy & the Gang)
- Zoe Shinno (and Midnite)
- Christine Sorenson
- Emily Stafford (and Randy & Pepper)
- Anne Teghtmeyer
- Lenai Waite (and Martin)
- Allison Walls (and Podo, Rue & Dom)
- Katie Williams
- Michele Zarichny

Gwen Cooper is the *New York Times* bestselling author of the memoirs *Homer's Odyssey: A Fearless Feline Tale, or How I Learned About Love and Life with a Blind Wonder Cat*; *Homer: The Ninth Life of a Blind Wonder Cat*; and *My Life in a Cat House: True Tales of Love, Laughter, and Living with Five Felines*, as well as the novel *Love Saves the Day*, narrated from a rescue cat's point of view. Her work has been published in more than two-dozen languages. She is a frequent speaker at shelter fundraisers and donates 10% of her royalties from *Homer's Odyssey* to organizations that serve abused, abandoned, and disabled animals.

Gwen lives in New Jersey with her husband, Laurence. She also lives with her two perfect cats—Clayton "the Tripod" and his litter-mate, Fanny—who aren't impressed with any of it.

**To learn more about Gwen and her books,
visit www.gwencooper.com**

Made in the USA
Middletown, DE
03 February 2024